Your Towns and Cities in the

Isle of Sheppey
in the Great War

Your Towns and Cities in the Great War

Isle of Sheppey
in the Great War

Stephen Wynn

Pen & Sword
MILITARY

First published in Great Britain in 2017 by
PEN & SWORD MILITARY
an imprint of
Pen and Sword Books Ltd
47 Church Street
Barnsley
South Yorkshire S70 2AS

Copyright © Stephen Wynn, 2017

ISBN 978 1 47383 406 4

The right of Stephen Wynn to be identified as the author of
this work has been asserted by him in accordance with the Copyright,
Designs and Patents Act 1988.

A CIP record for this book is available from the British Library

All rights reserved. No part of this book may be reproduced or transmitted
in any form or by any means, electronic or mechanical including
photocopying, recording or by any information storage and retrieval
system, without permission from the Publisher in writing.

Printed and bound in England
by CPI Group (UK) Ltd, Croydon, CR0 4YY

Typeset in Times New Roman by Chic Graphics

Pen & Sword Books Ltd incorporates the imprints of
Pen & Sword Archaeology, Atlas, Aviation, Battleground, Discovery,
Family History, History, Maritime, Military, Naval, Politics, Railways,
Select, Social History, Transport, True Crime, Claymore Press,
Frontline Books, Leo Cooper, Praetorian Press, Remember When,
Seaforth Publishing and Wharncliffe.

For a complete list of Pen and Sword titles please contact
Pen and Sword Books Limited
47 Church Street, Barnsley, South Yorkshire, S70 2AS, England
E-mail: enquiries@pen-and-sword.co.uk
Website: www.pen-and-sword.co.uk

Contents

	Author's Biography	6
1	Brief History of the Isle of Sheppey	7
2	1914 – Starting Out	12
3	1915 – Deepening Conflict	26
4	1916 – The Realisation	54
5	1917 – Seeing it through	80
6	1918 – The Final Blow	98
7	Those Who Didn't Come Home	121
8	The Aftermath	137
	Sources	156
	Index	157

Author's Biography

Stephen is a happily retired police officer, having served with Essex Police as a constable for thirty years between 1983 and 2013. He is married to Tanya who is also his best friend.

Both his sons, Luke and Ross, were members of the armed forces, collectively serving five tours of Afghanistan between 2008 and 2013. Both were injured on their first tour. This led to his first book, *Two Sons in a Warzone – Afghanistan: The True Story of a Father's Conflict*, which was published in October 2010.

His teenage daughter, Aimee, currently attends one of the District's secondary schools. Both of his grandfathers served in and survived the First World War, one with the Royal Irish Rifles, the other in the Mercantile Navy, while his father was a member of the Royal Army Ordnance Corp during the Second World War.

Stephen collaborated with one of his writing partners, Ken Porter, on a previous book published in August 2012, *German POW Camp 266 – Langdon Hills*, which spent six weeks as the number one best-selling book in Waterstones, Basildon, between March and April 2013. Steve and Ken collaborated on a further four books in the Towns & Cities in the Great War series by Pen and Sword. Stephen has also written other titles for the same series of books.

Stephen has also co-written three crime thrillers which were published between 2010 and 2012, and centre around a fictional detective named Terry Danvers.

When he is not writing, Tanya and he enjoy the simplicity of walking their four German Shepherd dogs early each morning when most sensible people are still fast asleep in their beds.

CHAPTER 1

Brief History of the Isle of Sheppey

The Isle of Sheppey is an island on the north coast of Kent and to the east of London overlooking both the Thames estuary and the River Medway.

The name *Sheppey* is derived from the ancient Saxon word *Screapige*, which when translated means Isle of Sheep. The connection is still in existence to this day with large flocks of sheep still grazed on the island's pastures.

There is evidence to support Neolithic and prehistoric occupation of the area, and the island was occupied in Roman and medieval times. In the year 855, the Isle of Sheppey became home to an invading Viking army, who used it as their base for the winter.

The island is separated from the rest of Kent by the Swale channel, which was used for shipping in ancient times, especially during times of bad weather, as it acted as a natural buffer to the dangers of having to manoeuvre in the waters of the Thames estuary or the North Sea.

During the sixteenth century, King Henry Vlll, having realised the strategic value of Sheerness, had a blockhouse built there along with two other similar fortifications on the island.

In 1666, Sir Bernard de Gomme, a Dutch engineer who had been knighted six years earlier, was sent to Sheerness by King Charles ll to review its fortifications and a fort was added to protect and strengthen the already present blockhouse. Ironically in June 1667 the Isle of Sheppey suffered the ignominy of being occupied by the Dutch for a week. A Dutch fleet of seventy-two ships sailed up the Thames estuary and captured the fort at Sheerness in a matter of a few hours.

The diary of Samuel Pepys states that the fort was manned largely by deserters from the British Royal Navy. Pepys at the time was the Secretary of the Navy Board. There was also the suggestion that those guarding the fort were simply soldiers who were underfed and unpaid, but whatever their status, they put up little in the way of a fight.

Before leaving, the Dutch pillaged supplies, ammunition and guns, before setting fire to most of the island's buildings. As a result of the Dutch 'invasion' and the ease and speed with which it was carried out, the importance of solid and dependable fortifications became obvious. But it was still nearly twenty years until they were finally completed.

As the dockyard at Sheerness increased in size and importance so did the defensive fortifications which surrounded it. After all, there would be no point in having a dockyard, where ships of the British Royal Navy could anchor up, be repaired and built, if it was vulnerable to attack by foreign fleets.

There was a later and much bigger structure, named Fort Townshend, built on the same site between 1780 and 1782, its main purpose being to defend Sheerness Dockyard.

On 16 April 1797, at Spithead, which was an anchorage location off Portsmouth, sailors and some officers on board sixteen British Royal Navy ships that were part of the Channel Fleet took the drastic step of demanding more pay and better living conditions on board the vessels on which they served.

Inspired by this, sailors on board ships at the Nore anchorage point, situated in the Thames estuary, mutinied on 12 May 1797. The British Royal Navy vessel, HMS *Sandwich*, was seized by her crew, which led other ships also anchored there to do the same, their grievances being the same as those of their comrades at Portsmouth.

A list of demands was delivered to Admiral Charles Buckner on 20 May 1797 which included asking for a pay rise, pardons for all and a modification of the navy's articles of war. For some reason the mutineers then added the addendum that the king, George III, dissolve Parliament and make peace with France, whom England was at war with at the time. Nearly all of the demands were refused other than pardons, which was on the understanding that the men returned to their normal duty immediately. Rather than accept this offer the mutineers decided to extend their activities; they blockaded London and prevented merchant ships from entering the capital to unload their cargoes. More and more of the ships which had been part of the original mutiny off the Isle of Sheppey sailed off, reducing the effectiveness of those who remained steadfast in their aims. The mutiny finally came to an end on 16 June 1797. The leader of the mutineers, Richard Parker, a sailor serving on board HMS *Sandwich,* along with twenty-eight others, were hanged on 30 June 1797 for their part, while others were imprisoned, sent to Australia or flogged.

Over time there have been different ferry services that have provided passage on and off the island for people and goods, but the last of these, the Harty Ferry, which provided a service to and from Faversham, stopped using the route before the beginning of the First World War. At about this time there was a passenger ferry service that operated between the Isle of Sheppey and the Dutch port of Flushing, as well as a mail service to Germany. With the outbreak of the war, both routes ceased.

The first two bridges connecting the island to the mainland of Kent were built by railway companies. The first, which opened for business on 19 July 1860, was erected by the London, Chatham and Dover Railway Company, before being replaced by one built by the South Eastern and Chatham Railway. This one opened for business on 6 November 1906.

During the First World War, the Isle of Sheppey wasn't a heavily populated area, but it still played an important part in the nation's war effort. It was one of only two designated military areas in Kent, and locally it acquired the name of the 'Barbed Wire Island'.

Its main claim to fame during the First World War would have to be in relation to aviation. In 1909 Lord Moore-Brabazon brought the Royal Aero Club to Leysdown, making it the first airfield in England. What became Eastchurch Aerodrome was where the first pilots of the Royal Naval Air Service were trained, making it the first military flying school. The Short Brothers also had an aircraft factory at Eastchurch, where they designed and built their own aircraft.

On 27 January 1912 in the Royal Aero Club newspaper, *Flight*, was the following brief article:

Naval Officers at Eastchurch
Lieut. C. R. Samson, RN, who has been in command of the Naval Flying establishment at Eastchurch, has been promoted to Acting Commander. This is the first promotion given to an officer in either service in connection with aviation.

One of those first pilots was a Lieutenant Charles Rumney Samson, who in July 1914 also became the officer commanding the Eastchurch (Mobile) Squadron, which in September 1914 was renamed No.3 Squadron, Royal Naval Air Service. Along with the rest of the squadron, he served both in France and the Dardanelles. He went on to become the first pilot to take off from a warship, as well as being the first to take off from a moving ship. He was also the first pilot to sink an aircraft carrier. He ended up with the rank of air commodore and was awarded the CMG, the DSO & Bar, the Air Force Cross, and the Croix de Guerre with palm. He was also made a Chevalier of the Legion d'Honneur.

There was also a balloon station at Sheerness, an emergency landing strip, another aircraft factory located at Shellbeach on the east coast of the island, as well as another emergency landing strip, at Harty in the south-east of the island.

The First World War added to the Isle of Sheppey's long and illustrious military history going back over hundreds of years. The part it played established the island's reputation for dogged determination to do what needed to be done for the greater good.

CHAPTER 2

1914
Starting Out

The *Dover Express* newspaper, in their edition for Friday, 1 May 1914, reported that permission had been sought to construct an explosives factory at Harty on the Isle of Sheppey. The selected site was about three miles away from the naval aerodrome and the Royal Aero Club's flying grounds at Eastchurch. The company, Messrs. Nobel Limited, applied to the Board of Trade for permission to construct two piers. One, of about 1,400 feet in length, would run south-east out from Bells Creek, which is situated at the western end of Harty. The second was to measure approximately 1,700 feet and run out west of the Ferry House at Harty, in a southerly direction, cutting across Lily Banks and into the channel of the Swale, before turning eastward and running parallel to the course of the channel for about 700 feet.

For the factory's production capability to be able to run at full capacity, 1,500 people would be required to work at the finished site.

On Saturday, 1 August 1914, just three days before the beginning of hostilities, the *Beverley and East Riding Recorder* reported that the Nobel Explosives Company's request had been refused by the Sittingbourne County Magistrates.

In the early days and weeks of the war everything was still quite surreal. Britain was at war with Germany, that much was known, but the war, other than being a word that meant death and destruction, didn't yet have any actual realism attached to it. People hadn't started receiving telegrams informing them of the death of a loved one, German air raids hadn't yet begun, returning wounded soldiers hadn't yet arrived back home, German prisoners of war hadn't been seen on British soil, and the booms of artillery bombardments couldn't be heard from across the English Channel. Life was continuing more or less as normal in towns, cities and villages up and down the country.

But with the war only a day old, the rumours of German spies being on the Isle of Sheppey had already gone into overdrive. At Sheerness Police Court on Wednesday, 5 August 1914, Franz Heinrich Losel, a 56-year-old German, was charged with suspected

Franz Heinrich Losel.

espionage. An unnamed soldier, a lance corporal, told the court that he saw Losel with a camera looking into the harbour at Sheerness where there were British Royal Navy ships at anchor. Losel denied that he was taking photographs. The case was adjourned so that the camera plates could be developed to see what they contained. Losel was remanded in custody for a week. It subsequently transpired that there were no images on any of the plates which Losel had in his possession at the time of his arrest.

On Friday, 14 August 1914, Losel was brought back before Sheerness Police Court where the charge against him was withdrawn. He was then immediately rearrested in the court under Section 12 of the Aliens Act, when he was informed that he was to be deported back to Germany. The warrant for his arrest, which had been issued by the Home Secretary, directed that he should be taken to Maidstone Jail to await a ship that would convey him back to Germany. Losel was a photographer who had lived at 10 Beach Road, and the Recreation Ground, in Sheerness for more than forty years. He was a single man who had been born in Saxony, Germany, in 1858.

It was reported in the *Whitstable Times & Herne Bay Herald* on 8 August 1914 that a man from Whitstable was seen sketching the Isle of Sheppey. He was also observed by a local boy scout to throw a piece of paper in to the sea. The boy scout took it upon himself to dive in to the sea to recover the discarded paper, which just happened to have German writing on it. On closer inspection it was seen to have been dated 1911. Despite this, the man was subsequently found by the police. He turned out to be an Englishman from Whitstable, an insurance agent by trade. Under the Defence of the Realm Act it was an offence to have in your possession a pen and paper in a public place, but he was found to have been simply engaging in his hobby of painting the landscape and was dealt with extremely lightly.

With the outbreak of war there were troop movements taking place all over the country. The Isle of Sheppey was one of the locations to which some of these troops were sent. The 8th

Battalion, Middlesex Regiment, which was a Territorial Unit, found themselves being sent to Sheppey with only a few hours' notice during the early days of the war, arriving there in about the second week of August. A body of men, numbering some 1,000 in total and led by Lieutenant Colonel W. Garner, arrived at Sheerness in readiness for any work, either at home or abroad, that they might be tasked with. One of the battalion's soldiers wrote a letter home to his family; it read as follows:

Just a line to let you know all's well. We are having a fine time on this island (the Isle of Sheppey). We have four companies here, and the other half are at Sheerness Barracks guarding German prisoners. Better here than at camp. This is all for this time. Good luck.

As this letter had been sent less than a week in to the war it is unclear who the prisoners were that were being held at Sheerness Barracks; maybe they were German civilians who had been interned.

The first British soldiers of the British Expeditionary Force left for France on 9 August 1914 to join up with their French and Belgian counterparts in an effort to stop the German 1st Army advancing along the Franco-German and Franco-Belgian borders. The area that had been allocated for the British to defend was from Alsace Lorraine to Mons and Charleroi. The British Forces were under the leadership of Field Marshal Sir John French, the commander-in-chief, and Sir Horace Smith-Dorrien who commanded the British Second Corps. An interesting point to note was that the two men were not the best of friends and hadn't been for many years.

The British Expeditionary Force which arrived at Mons on 22 August 1914, in readiness for what would be their first battle of the war, numbered some 80,000 men, a mixture of full-time professional soldiers and reservists, some of whom who had served in previous conflicts. The British were up against an enemy force estimated at double their size: 160,000 men. The total manpower of the German army at the start of the war was over one million men, as was that of the French.

On the same day that the British arrived at Mons, already weary from a long march, the French, in the shape of their Fifth Army, who were under the command of General Charles Lanrezac, were already fighting against the German Second and Third Army groups. The British Forces, centred at Mons, had no alternative but to take up defensive positions along the canal which ran through Mons from the directions of Conde and Charleroi, an area which included having to defend four bridges.

The Battle of Mons and the subsequent British retreat was the first of the war. It began in the afternoon of 23 August. The British had already incurred some heavy casualties and the French Fifth Army had begun to retreat which had dangerously exposed the British right flank to the advancing German forces. The retreat didn't stop until the outset of the Battle of the Marne which took place between 5 and 12 September 1914. This took place on the eastern outskirts of Paris and is where French and British forces made a concerted effort to stop the German advance.

From the outbreak of war up until the end of 1914, at least fifteen men from, or with connections to, Sheerness were killed or died as a result of their involvement in the war. Twelve of these were from the Royal Navy. One was killed with the sinking of HMS *Pathfinder* on 5 September. Four were killed with HMS *Aboukir*, three with HMS *Hogue* and one with HMS *Cressy*, all of which were sunk on 22 September 1914. And three men died with HMS *Hawke,* which was sunk by the German submarine *U-9* on 15 October 1914.

Three soldiers were killed during this time. The first was James Daniel Boother, aged 28 and a Private (L/7860) in the 1st Battalion, (Queen's Own Royal West Kent Regiment). He was killed in action during fighting on 23 September in what would have more than likely been the Battle of the Aisne. James had already enlisted in the army well before the outbreak of war. The 1911 census records that he was in the Regiment's 2nd Battalion, stationed in India. The war diaries for this battalion don't have a single entry for 23

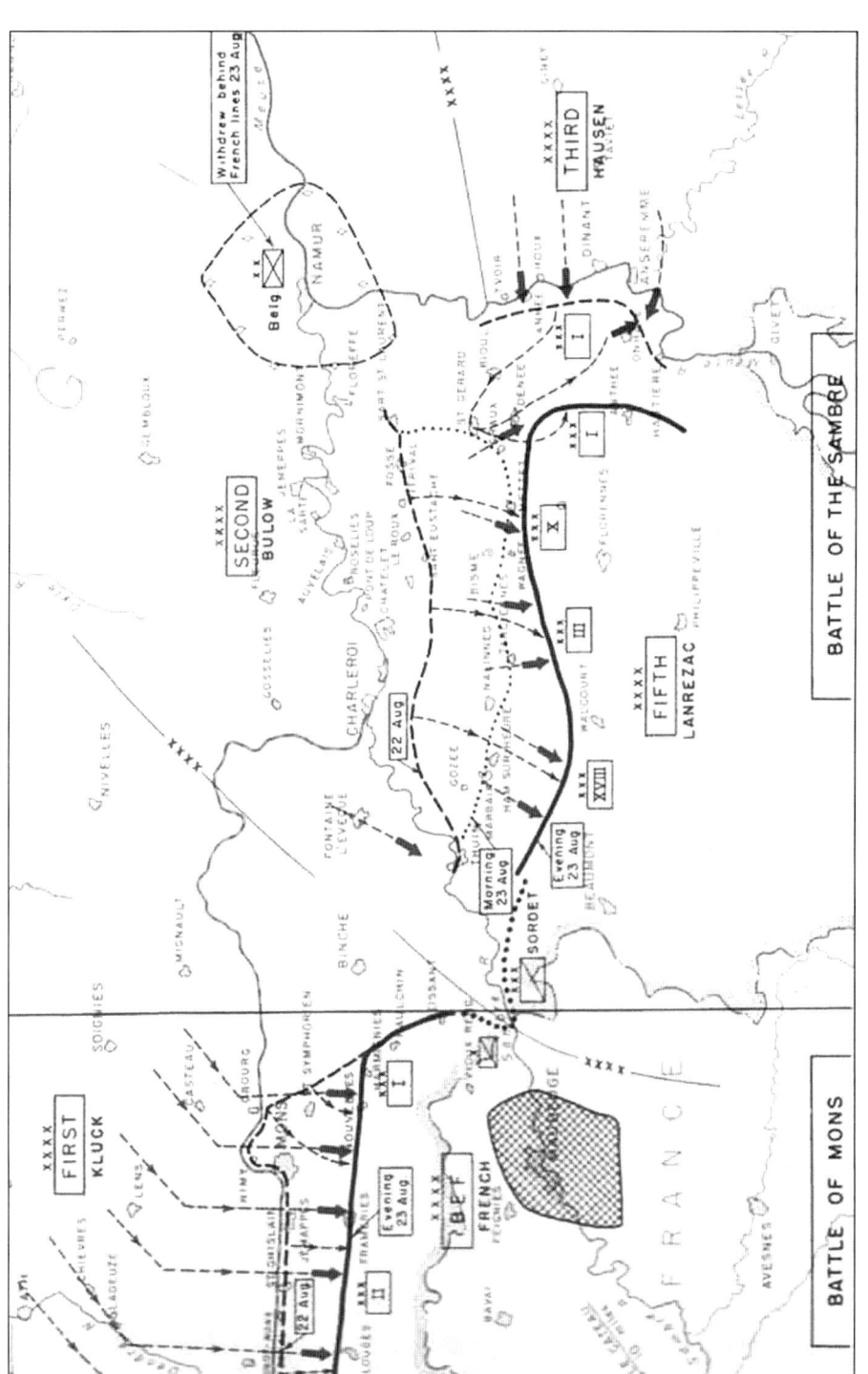

Map of the Battle of Mons.

September, but rather a combined entry for the period of 13 to 30 September 1914. It does however clearly show that the battalion was in trenches at Missy-sur-Aisne between those dates. It also included the following paragraph:

The total casualties of the battalion, since the campaign started, are at the end of the month, 61 killed, 178 wounded, 41 wounded and missing, 110 missing and 40 to hospital. Of these, 31 killed and 96 wounded occurred while the battalion was in occupation of the trenches at Missy-sur-Aisne.

It would appear that Boother's death came about while his battalion were occupying these trenches. Sadly, war diaries very rarely named men from the 'other ranks'. He has no known grave but his name is commemorated on the La Ferte-sous-Jouarre Memorial in the Seine-et-Marne region of France. After the war his mother Margaret Boother was, according to the Commonwealth War Graves Commission, living at 3 Kent Street, Blue Town, Sheerness, while the De Ruvigny's Roll of Honour for the period 1914-20 shows his father, George Boother, living at 25 Short Street, Sheerness, Isle of Sheppey.

Ernest George Carpenter was 33 years of age, having been born in Sheerness in 1892. He was a career soldier and a Private (8083) in the 2nd Battalion, Oxford and Bucks Light Infantry and was killed in action on 21 October 1914. He has no known grave and his name is commemorated on Ypres (Menin Gate) Memorial. The 1911 census shows that he was already serving in the army with the regiment's 1st Battalion and stationed in India. He had in fact enlisted in the army at Sheerness on 6 November 1905. Prior to enlisting he had been a carpenter by trade. His parents, Samuel and Agnes Carpenter, lived at 26 Maple Street, Sheerness, Isle of Sheppey, with Ernest's elder sister, Florence. The war diaries for the 2nd Battalion record their activities of 12 September 1914 when they moved from Beugneux on to Viel-Arcy, a distance of some sixteen miles. This was recorded on page 100 of the diary, but the next page of the diary jumps to 22 October 1914, the day after Ernest had been killed.

Alfred Charles Percival, who was 29 years of age and a private (9713) in the 1st Battalion, Northumberland Regiment, was killed in action on 27 October 1914 during the fighting of the Battle of Neuve Chapelle. He has no known grave and his name is commemorated on Le Tournet Memorial in the Pas-de-Calais region of France. The memorial contains the names of some 13,400 British soldiers who were killed in that region between the end of October 1914 and the end of September 1915 leading up to the Battle of Loos. Percival's widow, Agnes Harriet, lived at 45 Galway Road, Sheerness, Isle of Sheppey, with their two young children, Ronald and Josephine. The 1911 census showed the family living at 6 Hope Cottages, High Street, Chalvey, Slough, and Alfred's occupation as a groom. Alfred and Agnes were married on 24 December 1906 at the parish church in Burnham, Buckinghamshire.

As far as I have been able to establish, the first casualty of the war who had any connection with the Isle of Sheppey was Edward James Baker, a 37-year-old married man, whose father George lived in Sheerness. Edward was a petty officer 1st class and was on board HMS *Pathfinder* when she was sunk by the German submarine *U-21* on 5 September 1914 off the Berwickshire coastline of Scotland. Out of a ship's complement of 270 officers and men, there were only 11 survivors from the *Pathfinder*. Her loss was also a historic event as it earned her the unwelcome distinction of becoming the first ever warship to be sunk by a German submarine.

With the sinking of HMS *Aboukir*, HMS *Cressy* and HMS *Hogue* by the German submarine *U-9* while on patrol in the North Sea on 22 September 1914, the Isle of Sheppey lost a further eight men who had connections with the town.

The first soldier from the Isle of Sheppey to be killed during the First World War appears to have been 37-year-old Captain John Kenneth Tulloch Whish of the 1st Battalion, East Surrey Regiment, when he was killed in action on 8 September 1914. He is buried at the Perreuse Chateau Franco British National Cemetery, Seine-et-

Marne, France. John had joined the East Surrey Regiment in 1899 and had served in the Second Boer War (1899-1902) where he was twice mentioned in despatches, and the Nandi Expedition where he served with the 3rd King's African Rifles. He was the son of the late Colonel J.T. and Mrs M.B. Whish of 'Haven Cottage', Leysdown.

It was widely reported in the press at the end of September 1914 that letters had been sent to a number of German spies living at both Chatham and Sheerness. Under the powers which the Post Office authorities possessed to intercept, read and copy suspicious mail under wartime legislation, they opened all of the letters concerned and recorded their contents, before allowing the letters to be delivered to their intended recipients. In the main the letters were found to contain references to locations across the United Kingdom that were of particular interest to the German authorities. Some of the letters even asked the recipient to keep an eye on and find out as much as they could about certain named prominent British individuals, some of whom were thought to be members of the Intelligence Department of the War Office.

This led to a court case. The man in the dock was Karl Gustav Ernst. He was originally arrested on 4 August 1914, the day war broke out. He was initially dealt with under the Aliens Restriction Act. A warrant was issued by the Home Secretary for his deportation, but he was then brought up on spying charges which could be easily proved against him. In essence he received letters from his controller in Germany, which he then forwarded on to other individuals spying for Germany. At least one of these individuals lived in Sheerness.

On Tuesday, 20 October 1914, a massive fire broke out in the High Street, Blue Town, on the island immediately opposite the Dockyard wall. How it started isn't absolutely clear but it resulted in the destruction of a public house, a tobacconist's, and the Gordon Sailors Rest. The fact that more premises weren't destroyed in the fire was largely down to the large numbers of military personnel who were in residence on the island for one reason or another. Captain Prendergast, who was the superintendent of Sheerness

Dockyard, Colonel Percival who was the commanding officer of the Royal Engineers on the island, and officers and men under their command were able to attend the blaze quickly and initially contain the fire. Then when the Sheerness Dockyard Police Fire Brigade and the local council's Fire Brigade arrived, they put the fire out.

Blue Town, which acquired its name sometime in the early 1700s, came about due to the colour that dockyard workers painted the roofs of their properties. These were hard men, and they had to be, because Blue Town wasn't the most salubrious of locations and fighting was an everyday occurrence. But in a High Street which had its fair share of public houses, this hardly came as too much of a shock. As the working day finished, so the dockyards at Sheerness emptied and the pubs quickly started filling up, as men rushed to quench their thirst.

With the war only three months old, the decision was taken to close the Sheerness railway station to passenger traffic from Saturday, 7 November 1914 for the duration of the war. It was however still used for goods traffic. All passenger movements on and off the island were moved to Sheerness Dockyard railway station.

The inhabitants of the Isle of Sheppey were officially informed that as from 10 November 1914 a system of passports would come into operation which in essence would affect their freedom of movement on and off the island. The townspeople had seen notices in relation to the same posted on 1 November, but these were subsequently withdrawn, as the original conditions were revised having been thought to have been too stringent. On the original notices, people who wished to leave the island past the military canal were required to obtain a pass, but it was intimated that such passes would only be granted in limited numbers. If this had gone ahead, it could have ended up making some of the people virtual prisoners in their own homes.

The new order issued by the Chief Constable of Kent, Colonel Warde, came in to effect on Thursday, 12 November 1914. It stated that residents of Sheppey who wanted to leave the island by road

Permit for the Isle of Sheppey.

required an official pass to do so. Not surprisingly there was a massive demand for these passes. The police station on the island was besieged by those wanting to apply. The demand became so great that a number of military clerks had to be brought in to keep up with all of the paperwork involved.

On Thursday, 26 November 1914, tragedy struck when the Royal Navy Battleship HMS *Bulwark*, which was part of the 5th Battle Squadron, assigned to the Channel Fleet, blew up while anchored at buoy number seventeen in Keyhole Reach to the west of Sheerness. Besides the 736 ship's officers and crew who were killed in the initial explosion, another man died of his wounds the following day. Another died on 28 November, as did another on 29 November. Two died on 30 November, and the last of the crew to die did so more than three years later, on 18 January 1918. Although it was hard to believe that anybody could have survived the massive explosion, nine members of the crew actually did. They were:

Budd, Sergeant PO 8314, Albert Cosham
Day, Stoker 2nd Class K 21477, William Ewart Gladstone
Duffy, Stoker 1st Class K 17693, Fred Goodlad
Johnson, Leading Seaman 198355, William
Marshall, Able Seaman 231657, Stephen Frederick
Pitter, Able Seaman J 7172, Charles
Spackman, Able Seaman 205028, Frederick Charles
Strait, Able Seaman 226097, James
Stroud, Able seaman 161786, Norman

The 5th Battle Squadron had been transferred to Sheerness on 14 November 1914. Before she sank, the *Bulwark* had been busy loading ammunition. The exact reason for the explosion that tore her apart is not clear, but a naval court of enquiry which sat on 28 November 1914 stated that the most likely scenario was that the artillery shells brought onto the ship had been stacked too tightly and too close to the hot metal of the ship's boilers, causing some of them to ignite and explode, setting off the others which in turn led to the sinking of the ship and the tragically high loss of life.

So powerful was the explosion that a large section of the ship was literally blown to pieces. Years later when divers went down to locate her position on the sea bed, all they could find was the ship's port bow which lay some fifty feet east of her mooring, and the starboard bow which lay a further thirty feet away. What remains of HMS *Bulwark* on the bottom of the seabed now comes under the Protection of the Military Remains Act.

Christmas Day 1914 was memorable for the people of the Isle of Sheppey, and especially those living in Sheerness. Not only was it the first Christmas of the war, but just as residents of the town were sitting down for their Christmas dinner, the following announcement was made by the Secretary of the War Office:

> *A hostile aeroplane was sighted today at 1235 pm flying very high east to west over Sheerness. British aircraft went up in pursuit and engaged the enemy, who, after being hit three or four times, was driven off.*

The aircraft concerned was believed to be a Taube and after flying over Sheerness it headed at great speed in the general direction of Essex and Shoeburyness, presumably on route back to its home base. Three British aircraft from the Royal Flying Corps took to the skies in hot pursuit of the German aircraft, but to no avail, as it was more than able to outfly them. Attempts from anti-aircraft guns to assist, although well intentioned, were futile due to the range.

The Taube was a German monoplane which had been in production since before the war and was her first mass-produced military aircraft. It was used as a fighter, a bomber, for surveillance and for training purposes. Ironically, just six months into the war the Taube was removed from frontline service due to its poor manoeuvrability and its perceived lack of speed.

The festive attack by the German aircraft led to both the Admiralty and the War Office taking the unprecedented steps of issuing warnings to the public as to the dangers they faced from the 'projectiles' that were being fired at enemy aircraft by 'our own guns'. Prior to this, the British government had been more concerned about not spreading panic and fear amongst the civilian population and about the effect which such warnings might have on their morale, than they were about furnishing them with cold hard facts on how best to protect themselves against this previously unthought-of threat to public safety. But it was a real danger. Warning sirens were not in place back in 1915, so it was more than feasible that the streets of the towns in the Isle of Sheppey could be busy with people going about their everyday business when an air raid took place, which meant there was a risk of injury to civilians from falling ground-fired projectiles that, having missed their intended targets, returned back down to earth.

CHAPTER 3

1915
Deepening Conflict

With the war not being over, as some had predicted it would be by Christmas of 1914, there was a fear, maybe even a belief, especially amongst some politicians, that in an effort to break the stalemate which had enveloped the Western Front, the Kaiser would send his armies across the channel to invade Great Britain. This would have not only resulted in British and Allied troops having to be withdrawn from the fighting in France and Belgium, but it would have brought the war directly to the very epicentre of the British Empire.

The shortest and least dangerous route across the English Channel for an invading army from Europe would see them landing somewhere on the coastline of Kent. There was of course the option of sailing up the River Thames, straight into the heart of London, but with the defences in place on both the Kent and Essex sides of the river, this was an unlikely option.

So the Isle of Sheppey became a massive defensive fortress, not only to prevent any German landing, but also to help protect the naval dockyards at Chatham and Sheerness. As part of the defences to protect against German submarines, a boom system ran between Garrison Point Fort at Sheerness across to what was known as the grain tower on the Isle of Grain. Along the entire stretch of the seaward side of the Isle of Sheppey, a series of defensive structures were put in place. Collectively they were so impressive, almost to the point of impregnability, that an attempted landing anywhere along this stretch of coastline would have been almost suicidal.

The nickname 'Barbed Wire Island' was an apt title during the First World War for the Isle of Sheppey. Firstly, any invaders would have to get ashore while under heavy fire from the island's gun batteries and machine gun positions which were safely ensconced inside reinforced concrete pillboxes. If they survived getting ashore they then had to contend with the lines of barbed wire that was waiting for them. Beyond this there were trenches and large earthen redoubts. Although an impressive defensive system, it was thankfully never put to the test.

The major battles of 1915 took place at Gallipoli, Ypres, Neuve Chapelle, and Loos, the latter of which saw the first use of poison gas by the British army on 25 September. There was also the naval battle at Dogger Bank between the British and German navies, and on 19 December Douglas Haig replaced Sir John French as the commander of the British Expeditionary Force. The year was also notable for the first German Zeppelin raid on mainland Britain, when the *L3* airship dropped ten bombs on Great Yarmouth on 19 January, a raid in which two people were killed. It was also the year that saw the first use of chlorine gas by the German army, when they released over 5,000 cylinders of the gas at Langemark in Flanders at the beginning of the Second Battle of Ypres on 22 April. May 5 saw the sinking of the *Lusitania* in a German U-boat attack; more than 1,200 people lost their lives when the ship sunk, including 128 Americans. This would eventually be one of the reasons why America came in to the war on the side of Britain and her allies in April 1917.

It would also be a year in which seventy-two men from the Isle of Sheppey were killed or died as a result of their involvement in the war. However, carrying out the research to arrive at that number wasn't as straight forward as it would at first appear. Let me explain.

When searching on the Commonwealth War Graves Commission website, I placed in the 'Additional Information' box the town name,

Sheerness. That came up with a total of sixty-four men who had been killed or died of their wounds throughout the course of 1915 and who had connections with the town. This included forty-six civilian dockyard workers who died in the explosion and sinking of HMS *Princess Irene* on 27 May 1915. I have named and written about these men elsewhere in the book. Below are the details of the remaining eighteen men:

William George Brunger was born in Minster on the Isle of Sheppey on 16 March 1880. He was a married man. His widow, Gertrude Florence, lived at 309 High Street, Sheerness. His parents, Simon and Edith, also lived in the town, although according to the 1911 census William and Gertrude were at the time living at 111 Livingstone Road, Gillingham, Kent.

William had long ago decided that it was to be a life on the ocean wave for him, and he joined the Royal Navy on 16 March 1898, initially signing on for twelve years. Having completed his service, he decided to continue his career in the navy, especially as by then he had become a chief writer (340584). He was serving on board HMS *Goliath*, a Canopus class pre-dreadnought battleship, which in the years immediately before the start of the First World War had been in 'mothballs' gathering dust and cobwebs. In March 1915, *Goliath*, having been recommissioned, was sent out to take part in the Dardanelles campaign and took part in the Gallipoli landings the following month. While on patrol in Morto Bay off the coast of Cape Helles on 13 May 1915, she was attacked by the Turkish torpedo boat *Muavenet-I Milliye* and sunk when two torpedoes struck her. Out of a crew of 700 officers and men, 570 were either killed in the explosion or drowned, including William George Brunger. His body was not recovered and his name is commemorated on the Chatham Naval Memorial. Two of William's brothers, Augustus and Henry, also served in the Royal Navy.

Ernest Steele had first enlisted in the army as private (L/9898) on 13 November 1912 when he was a month shy of his eighteenth birthday. He had been a baker in Harbledown, near Canterbury, prior to becoming a soldier. He was initially allocated to the 3rd (Reserve) Battalion, The Buffs, before transferring to the Regiment's 1st Battalion at a later date. Four months before enlisting in the regular army he had been accepted in to the Army Reserve, signing up on 10 July 1912 at Canterbury as Private 10293. There was initially some concern as to Ernest's age when he applied to join the Army Reserve. His father Joseph received an army Form C.348, more commonly known as a memorandum, dated 10 July 1912. It read as follows:

> *Dear Sir,*
> *Your son presented himself for enlistment yesterday and stated his age to be 17 years and 7 months, will you please forward birth certificate for verification.*
> *This will be returned to you immediately.*
> *B. Rumley*
> *Sergeant.*

At the time the Steele family were living at 14 Orchard Place, Faversham, Kent. Joseph Steele's reply was as follows:

> *Sir,*
> *I cannot find birth certificate of my son Ernest Steele at present, but he was born on 24th November 1894.*
> *Yours respectfully*
> *Joseph Steele*
> *Late*
> *Band King's Dragoon Guards.*

It can only be assumed that the army's concerns about Ernest's age had been suitably addressed by his father's response, as he was accepted in to the Army Reserve as from 10 July 1912.

While his battalion was in Ireland during the first half of 1914, Ernest suffered the consequences of three breaches of army discipline. The first occasion was on 23 February 1914 while his battalion were stationed at Fermoy. He was charged with not complying with an order given by an NCO. He was found guilty and his punishment was 'confined to barracks for three days'. His second offence was also while he was stationed at Fermoy, and this time it was for being 'absent from school'. This saw him confined to barracks for a further eight days. His third and final transgression took place on 20 May 1914 while he was stationed at Kilworth, when he was charged with having 'dirty equipment'. He was found guilty and his punishment was to be confined to his company for three days.

Ernest first arrived in France on 7 September 1914. On 14 February 1915 his battalion was involved in fighting when he received a gunshot wound to the head. He was initially treated at No.17 Field Ambulance. From there he was transferred to No. 2 Casualty Clearing Station, before ending up at No. 11 General Hospital in Boulogne, where he subsequently died of his wounds on 15 March 1915.

He is buried at the Boulogne Eastern Cemetery in the Pas-de-Calais. At the time of Ernest's death, his home address was Beaulieu, Sheerness East, Isle of Sheppey. The Infantry Records Office at Hounslow had Ernest's next of kin shown as being Mrs Polly E. Steele of Little Rydes Farm, Eastchurch. They returned the following items to her which were Ernest's personal effects:

> 6 letters (presumably from Polly)
> 2 photos
> 1 (writing) pad

John William Argent was also a private (L/8566) in the 1st Battalion of The Buffs (East Kent Regiment) when he was killed in action on 19 July 1915. He is buried at La Brique Military Cemetery the West-Vlaanderen (West Flanders) region of Belgium. His parents, William and Ellen Argent, lived in Sheerness.

Albert Batt was 25 years of age and a private (8942) in the 1st Battalion, Royal Welsh Fusiliers, when he died of his wounds on 2

July 1915. He is buried at the Netley Military Cemetery in Hampshire. His parents, Alfred and Fanny Batt, lived 110 Invicta Road, Sheerness, Isle of Sheppey

George Richardson was 29 years of age and a carpenter's mate (343606) in the Royal Navy and was serving on board HMS *Formidable* when she was sunk by two torpedoes fired by an unknown German submarine on 1 January 1915 while on exercise in the English Channel. This made her only the second battleship of the Royal Navy to be sunk as a result of enemy action during the First World War. The *Formidable* was part of the Royal Navy's 5th Battle Squadron which at the time was stationed at Sheerness, its main function being to help prevent a German invasion of the United Kingdom. Out of a ship's complement of 780 officers and men, there were only 133 survivors. George Richardson was one of those who perished. He has no known resting place and his name is commemorated on the Chatham Naval Memorial. His parents lived at 126 Berridge Road, Sheerness, Isle of Sheppey.

Edward Thompson was 37 years of age and a petty officer (181978) in the Royal Navy, serving on HMS *Clan McNaughton*, an auxiliary cruiser, when the ship was lost in extremely bad weather off the north coast of Ireland on 3 February 1915. Her crew of 280 officers and men were all lost, presumed drowned. Thompson's body was not recovered and his name is commemorated on the Chatham Naval Memorial. His widow, Mrs L.E. Thompson, lived at 25 Maple Street, Sheerness, on the Isle of Sheppey.

Frederick George Cox was only 17 years of age, a boy 1st class (J/24709) in the Royal Navy, and part of the crew of HMS *Clan McNaughton* that was lost when she sank on 3 February 1915. His name is also commemorated on the Chatham Naval Memorial. His parents, Frederick and Sarah Cox, lived at 2 Acorn Street, Mile Town, Sheerness, Isle of Sheppey.

Arthur Septimus Hamnett was an able seaman (216503) in the Royal Navy, serving at HMS *Pembroke* base at Chatham when he died due to illness on 17 February 1915. He was buried at the Woodlands Cemetery in Gillingham at Kent. His widow lived at 10 Fonblanque Road, Marine Town, Isle of Sheppey.

Ernest Foster George was 23 years of age and a local man, born in Sheerness. He was a shipwright 2nd class (M/6777) in the Royal Navy and was stationed at the shore base of HMS *Pembroke* when he died on 12 July 1915. He is buried in the Woodlands Cemetery at Gillingham, Kent. His parents, Ernest and Nellie, lived at 'Garthowen', 73 High Street, Stourbridge.

Edwin Austin Sullivan was 18 years of age and a private (1369) in the 5th Battalion, Australian Infantry, when he was killed in action during fighting at Gallipoli on 8 May 1915. He has no known grave and his name is commemorated on the Helles Memorial, which is situated on the Gallipoli Peninsula.

Edwin's father Dennis, who was widowed, lived at 101 James Street, Sheerness on the Isle of Sheppey. He was a naval pensioner, having been a chief gunner in the Royal Marines. Edward had two elder sisters, Margaret and Monah.

Robert Gordon was 21 years of age and a private (3159) in the 4th Battalion, Seaforth Highlanders, when he was killed in action during fighting on the Western Front on 9 May 1915. His name is commemorated on the Le Touret Memorial in the Pas-de-Calais. His mother, Mrs A. Gordon, lived at Southdown Road, Halfway, Sheerness.

William John Henry Reed was born in Sheerness in 1894. With the outbreak of the First World War he enlisted in the army, becoming an acting bombardier in the Royal Field Artillery. He was killed in action on 5 September 1915. He is buried at the Divisional Cemetery which can be found about a mile west of the Belgian town of Ieper, West-Vlaanderen. The 1901 census shows William and his parents, John and Francis, living at 49 Unity Street, Sheerness, but ten years later they were living at 38 Elder Street in Brighton.

Alexander Mackintosh Wilson was 26 years of age and a petty officer (236498) in the Royal Navy. He was serving on HMS *Natal*,

HMS Natal.

a Warrior class cruiser, when he was killed on 30 December 1912 due to an internal explosion while the vessel was in the waters of the Cromarty Firth, where she was based as part of the British Navy's Second Cruiser Squadron.

On the afternoon of 30 December 1912, Captain Eric Black had arranged for a party on board HMS *Natal* for the wives and children of his officers, which included his own family, while it was at anchor in the Cromarty Firth. Some nurses from the hospital ship HMHS *Drina*, which was at anchor near the *Natal*, had also been invited. At about 3.30 pm the ship was rocked by a number of explosions at the rear of the ship. Confusion initially reigned, with some believing that the ship had either been torpedoed by a German submarine or had struck a mine. Some 400 of her crew and civilian visitors were

Upside down hull of HMS Natal.

killed in the tragedy. The *Natal* had a full complement of 712 officers and men. The subsequent enquiry in to the incident revealed that the *Natal* had suffered a catastrophic internal ammunition explosion, which was probably down to faulty cordite that had been stored in or near the small arms magazine. The remains of the wreck are today protected by the Protection of Military Remains Act 1986 as a designated wreck site.

Wilson's name is commemorated on the Chatham Naval Memorial. His parents, Alexander and Eliza, lived at 32 Granville Road, Sheerness, Isle of Sheppey.

George Hardy was 35 years of age and a private (3/8058) in the 1st Battalion, Norfolk Regiment, when he was killed in an accident on 20 October 1915. He is buried at the Villers-Bretonneux Military Cemetery, which is in the Somme region of France. His widow Laura lived at 113 Berridge Road in Sheerness, which made them neighbours of George Richardson who is mentioned earlier in this chapter.

William Hogben was 24 years of age and a private (751) in the

15th Battalion, Australian Infantry, when he died on 17 August 1915 of his wounds which he received during fierce fighting at Gallipoli. His name is commemorated on the Lone Pine Memorial which is incorporated in the Lone Pine Cemetery. William's parents, James and Clara, lived at 41 Marine Parade, Sheerness.

Thomas Henry Purdy was 40 years of age and a chief writer (173317) in the Royal Navy. He was serving on HMS *Formidable* when he was killed on 1 January 1915 when the battleship was sunk in the English Channel after being struck by two torpedoes fired from a German submarine. Thomas's parents, John and Isabella, were residents of Sheerness.

John Richard Bromley was 38 years of age and a ship's corporal 1st class in the Royal Navy. He was serving on board HMS *Natal* when the ship exploded on 30 December 1915 while at anchor at the Cromarty Firth. He was a holder of the China Medal 1900 and the Royal Navy's Long Service and Good Conduct Medal. His widow, Louise Bromley, lived at 71 Unity Street, Sheerness. His name is commemorated on the Chatham Naval Memorial.

George Thomas Paston was a leading seaman (221318) in the Royal Navy and serving on board HMS *Princess Irene*, a converted auxiliary minelayer, when she sank on 27 May 1915 after a massive internal explosion while at anchor off Sheerness, with the loss of 352 lives. The story of the *Princess Irene* will be told later in this book. George's widow Georgina lived at 7 Cross Street, Sheerness.

Frederick Charles Saunders was 34 years of age and a gunner (18423) in the 82nd Battery, Royal Garrison Artillery, 10th Brigade, when he died on 25 October 1915. He is buried at the Basra War Cemetery and had previously served in the South African campaign (1899-1902). He was born in Sheerness.

I then searched under 'Isle of Sheppey'. This brought up two names. The first was **Albert Victor Murdock**, who was a 21-year-old private (L/9394) in the 2nd Battalion, The Buffs (East Kent Regiment), killed on 28 May 1915. His home address was at 4 Coastguards Cottages, Leysdown, where he lived with his mother,

Elizabeth. The other individual was William Henry Castle, who was 19 years of age and a private (G/5462) in the 2nd Battalion, Queen's Own (Royal West Surrey Regiment), killed on 25 September 1915. He lived with his parents at 'Holmwood', Seathorpe Avenue, Minster, Isle of Sheppey.

Private Murdock also came up when I carried out a separate search under the town name of Leysdown and Private Castle's name also came up when I searched under the town of Minster.

A search of 'Blue Town' came up with just one name, that of James Brown, who was a civilian 'hired yard boy' who worked at HM Dockyard at Sheerness. He was just 15 years of age when he was killed on 27 May 1915, while helping with the loading of mines on to HMS *Princess Irene* when it exploded, killing nearly everybody on board. His body was never recovered and his name is commemorated on the Chatham Naval Memorial. His name is also included in the list of names that came up when I searched under 'Sheerness'. The Commonwealth War Graves Commission records that he lived with his parents, Isaiah and Elizabeth Mary Ann, his three brothers, Charles, Henry and Samuel, and a sister, Elizabeth, at 11 Sheppey Street, Blue Town. The 1911 census shows his mother's name as being Mary Ann Brown and the family living at 3 Sheppey Street.

A search for 'Eastchurch' also came up with just one name, that of **Alfred John William Newman**, who was a 19-year-old civilian shipwright apprentice, employed at HM Dockyard, Sheerness. He was also killed when HMS *Princess Irene* exploded off Sheerness on 27 May 1915. His parents, William and Clara, lived at Trout's Farm, Water Lane, Eastchurch, Isle of Sheppey, although the 1911 census shows the family home at 34 Hope Street, Sheerness.

A search for 'Marine Town' also came up with four names; these were included in the list for 'Sheerness'.

The last town name which I searched under for the Isle of Sheppey was Queenborough. This came up with five names, one of which had already come up when I searched under 'Marine Town'. This left the following four names:

Alfred William Sellen was 21 years of age and a private (9422) in the 2nd Battalion, East Yorkshire Regiment, when he died of his wounds on 24 February 1915. He is buried at the St Sever Cemetery in Rouen, Seine-Maritime, France. His parents, James and Fanny, lived in Queenborough on the Isle of Sheppey.

George Edward Knowler was only 18 years of age and a private (L/10483) in the 8th Battalion, Queen's Own (Royal West Kent Regiment), when he was killed in action on 16 October 1915, having first arrived in France less than a month before. He is buried in the Spoilbank Cemetery in West-Vlaanderen. He had enlisted on 1 September 1914 at Sheerness, soon after his eighteenth birthday. He lived with his parents, Thomas and Agnes, his four brothers, James, Herbert, Arthur and Wilfred, and three sisters, Blanche, Elizabeth and Doris, at 6 Woodhall Terrace, Queenborough. James spent four months in the Royal Navy between 10 January and 3 April 1915, and before the war he had been an apprentice engine fitter. Younger brother Herbert followed in the footsteps of James and joined the Royal Navy, where he spent nearly two years between 4 June 1917 and 18 April 1919.

Charles Beaumont was 26 years of age and a sergeant (1747) in the 2nd Battalion, Rifle Brigade, when he was killed in action on 10 May 1915. He has no known grave and his name is commemorated on the Ploegsteert Memorial. His parents, Robert and Emilie, and his three brothers, Robert, Henry and John, lived at 7 West Street, and 27 Castle Street, Queenborough. Robert had served in the Royal Navy for seven years between 19 May 1905 and 1 May 1912.

Frederick S. Wood was a yeoman of signals (CH/211530) in the British Royal Navy and serving on HMS *Pyramus* when he was killed in action on 9 September 1915. The ship had been on patrol in the Persian Gulf, ending up at Bushire, an area that was under attack from the Targistani tribe. In an effort to support the local inhabitants and in defence of the port, a landing party from the *Pyramus* was sent ashore on 8 September. The following day Wood and Chief Petty Officer Gentry were killed in the fighting. Both men were buried the following day, with their friends and comrades from the *Pyramus* in attendance. Frederick's parents, Frederick and Emily, lived at Coastguard House, Queensborough.

During the late 1800s and the early 1900s the country was awash with advertisements for medicines, linctuses, remedies, emulsions and potions that could cure every ailment known to man. One such advertisement, in the form of a supposed letter written in by a reader, appeared in the *Daily Record* on Tuesday, 9 February 1915. The only reason I determined to read through it was because the supposed writer who had penned the letter, extolling the virtues of this life-saving remedy, was from Minster on the Isle of Sheppey. Here is what the letter said:

> *Sirs,*
>
> *We have used Scott's Emulsion for fifteen years, with our family of eleven. Our twin children have been exceptionally delicate requiring the greatest care and I am quite sure that your wonderful Emulsion has been the means, with the blessing of God, of rearing these three sets of twins. The first twins were very weakly at birth. We commenced giving Scott's Emulsion, in small doses, when they were only one month, and as time went on they were little models. Then came a trying period which nearly cost them their lives. When they were only one year and seven months old. They were laid very low with sickness and diarrhoea, which reduced them to mere shadows. Just at this time, their twin brothers were born. Scott's Emulsion was administered again with the most gratifying results, gradually building up their wasted frames, restoring them once more to perfect health. Our little babies, Albert and Arthur, were our next trouble, Albert having rickets, we tried Scott's Emulsion with the same good results. Then as these dear children grew, whooping cough was the next trouble, there being five children all down with it. The eldest twins, James and John, being about five years had it most severe, and then again we thought we should have lost*

them. We tried different remedies, but we were only too glad to go back to the old remedy, 'Scott's.' We can truly say that again their health and strength was restored to them by the constant use of Scott's Emulsion. All our other children have also benefited, especially our two little girls who are much subject to bronchitis in the changeable weather we are so subject to. Our little baby girl is now trying it, with the most marked results. She has greatly surprised us all as people who saw her, never thought she would live. I am firmly convinced that we owe a debt of much gratitude to your famous medicine and shall always recommend its use in sickness of any kind. I must also add that occasionally I take it myself as I am not a strong woman.

Signed Ellen Amelia Matthews (A grateful mother)
Halfway House, Minster, nr Sheerness, Isle of Sheppey.

So that's Rickets, bronchitis, whooping cough, diarrhoea and general sickness it managed to cure. It also apparently worked wonders on colds, measles, weakness and debility, whatever the last two actually were. The main ingredient of the Emulsion appears to have been nothing more ingenious than cod liver oil, and although the advertisement did not say how much or what size bottles it came in, it did go to great lengths to encourage readers not to purchase cheaper cod liver oil preparations, as to do so could risk the health of their child.

Despite my doubts as to the authenticity of the Matthews family, they did actually exist. They had eleven children, which included three sets of twins, and they lived at Halfway House, Minster, near Sheerness, just as it said in the letter.

On Wednesday, 17 February 1915, a meeting took place of the Scout Association in the club room of the 1st Cranbrook Boy Scouts. The association's president, the Reverend H.P. Fitzpatrick, chaired the meeting. He began by saying that owing to the association's secretary having to rejoin the navy, normal day-to-day business had been somewhat delayed. The secretary's position had been taken by Mr Beeding who had agreed to accept the post of honorary secretary after he had been proposed by the president and seconded by Mr Hardcastle. After other similar positions were also filled, the evening's business began. Top of the agenda was the topic of coast patrol work. The chairman stated that a total of eight boys were needed for this duty on the Isle of Sheppey, and that three boys from the Goudhurst Troop had agreed to cover it. It was agreed to make up the required number from some of the association's other troops.

The Isle of Sheppey patrol would have been an interesting one for the teenage scouts who undertook it, what with barbed wire defences, gun emplacements and army camps in abundance.

An article appeared in the *Nottingham Evening Post* dated Tuesday, 23 February 1915, about Robert Stanley Harrison who had enlisted as a private in the Rifle Brigade in September 1914 and five months later had been promoted to the rank of second lieutenant and posted to the 14th Battalion, (Sherwood Foresters) Nottingham & Derbyshire Regiment. He had undergone all of his training on the Isle of Sheppey. His father was the Reverend Charles Harrison, who was the parish priest in the picturesque village of Selston in Nottingham. Robert had two brothers, Harold Charles Harrison, who was two years older than him and an engineer, and Ralph Collins Harrison, who was three years younger and a teacher. He also had a sister, Grace Mary Elliot, who was married to John Joseph Elliot, a chemist. Robert not only survived the war, but lived to the ripe old age of 92, passing away in June 1979 in Bournemouth.

What was originally reported as a German air raid over the Isle of Sheppey on the afternoon of Friday, 16 April 1915, turned out to be a single enemy aircraft. It flew low enough for those on the ground to see that it was a biplane and fitted with floats, indicating it was part of the Imperial German Airforce's seaplane section. Initially it appeared to be engaged in a scouting mission but, although the aircraft did not drop any bombs while it flew over the Isle of Sheppey, it did drop some on the outskirts of Faversham, which thankfully did not cause any major damage other than a fire in a meadow, suggesting that it might have been an incendiary device rather than an explosive bomb. One of the bombs landed close to a military hospital that at the time housed some thirty wounded British soldiers. Anti-aircraft units opened fire on the aircraft, but with no success in bringing it down, although it is believed that it was slightly damaged by the ground fire. Coupled with the sudden appearance of a British aircraft, this was sufficient to hasten its departure.

What was believed to be the same aircraft, later flew over Sittingbourne, some nine miles from Sheerness. It dropped one of its bombs, which landed in an orchard. Other than ruining one of the fruit trees and killing a blackbird it caused no major damage and nobody was injured or killed in the explosion. Still maintaining a high speed and keeping to a great height, the aircraft rapidly disappeared. A short while later it reappeared at a much lower elevation, which immediately attracted both rifle and machine gun fire from the ground. Whether the German aircraft knew its location at the time is unclear. As it was light at the time, it can only be assumed the pilot knew that by dropping his bombs where he did, he was unlikely to cause death or injury to those on the ground. British aircraft were not quick enough in their response to be able to challenge the aircraft as it made good its escape. The body of the solitary victim of the attack, the blackbird, was collected from the orchard, still warm, after the German aircraft had left.

HMS *Princess Irene* had started life as an ocean-going passenger liner for the Canadian Pacific Railway Company for use on the Vancouver–Victoria–Seattle route. She was launched on 20 October 1914, having been built by William Denny and brothers Ltd, of Dumbarton, Scotland.

At the outbreak of the war, she was requisitioned by the Admiralty and converted in to an auxiliary mine-laying vessel for the Royal Navy. At 11.14 am on Thursday, 27 May 1915, she exploded and what was left of the vessel sank while she was at anchor in the Medway Estuary off the Isle of Sheppey. A total of

HMS Princess Irene.

352 people, including 273 members of her crew and 76 dockyard workers from Chatham, lost their lives. She was being loaded with 500 mines in preparation for a deployment at the time of the explosion, which was so powerful it caused a column of flame some 300 feet in height. Besides those on board who perished, others who lived and worked in the surrounding area were killed from flying debris. One was a 9-year-old girl who lived on the Isle of Grain. Others included a farm labourer, who died of a heart attack, and the crew-member of a nearby ship who was killed when he was hit by a large piece of flying metal. There were reports of some of the debris landing up to twenty miles away. Three of the *Princess Irene*'s crew had a lucky escape as they were ashore at the time. Only one member of the crew is known to have survived the explosion: David Wills, one of the ship's stokers. He was found in the cold waters of the River Medway, having incurred severe burns. Many of the dead were literally blown to pieces, but the bodies that were recovered were buried at the Woodlands Road Cemetery in

nearby Gillingham. Identification was only possible in some of the cases because of names stitched into clothing or distinctive tattoos that were recognised by others.

On 31 May 1915 an inquest was opened on two of those who had died, with the coroner, Mr C.B. Harris, expressing his sympathies with those who had lost loved ones in the tragedy. He announced that subject to official approval, he proposed to take the same course of action as in the case of the HMS *Bulwark* disaster which, after a verdict had been given on just one of the victims, this same verdict would be accepted as the cause of death for everyone else killed in the disaster. This would obviate the need for a jury having to be called and inquests required each and every time a body or remains subsequently came to light. Looking at that decision through today's eyes it appears somewhat strange, as the cause of death of a washed-up body would not necessarily be the same as that of one that died in the explosion.

The inquest was on the bodies of George James Turner, a shipwright, and Victor Potter, who was 35 years of age and an electrical fitter. Turner was part of the group of dockyard workers who were on board the *Princess Irene* at the time of the explosion, while Potter died from injuries received by being struck by debris while on board a ship that was a thousand yards away. Giving evidence of identification in the case of Potter, a witness by the name of Leonard Himmerston, also an electrical fitter, told the inquest that he had heard the explosion of the *Princess Irene* and considered it far more violent than that of the HMS *Bulwark* which had occurred a few months earlier. Himmerston said that he had seen and recognised Potter's body at the naval hospital.

Harold James Wright, an engineer who was serving on board a coal depot vessel, said he was in his cabin when the explosion occurred. After the glass and debris on his vessel had stopped falling, he rushed up on deck and was just in time to see the remains of the *Princess Irene* floating on the water. He then saw Potter lying in the chart house of their vessel which was wrecked. After kicking the door in, he and his colleagues discovered Potter a short while later lying on the floor of the chart house. He indicated to them where he was injured, which was a somewhat remarkable feat taking into account how badly injured he was. A piece of metal which was subsequently found to weigh some seventy pounds, and is believed to have been a piece of the *Princess Irene*'s main beam, had smashed through the side of the chart house where Potter was sitting.

The coroner asked the jury to give a verdict in the case of Potter, and intimated that he proposed adjourning the inquest on Turner. The jury quickly returned a verdict that Potter's death was due to concussion and lacerations due to injuries received from an explosion through causes unascertained. The inquest on Turner was adjourned until 14 June.

Turner was buried at the Maidstone Road Cemetery in Chatham and Potter was buried at the South Ealing Cemetery. Four days after the explosion, a memorial service was held at the dockyard church in Sheerness which was taken by the Archbishop of Canterbury, Randall Davidson.

A court of enquiry was held into the tragedy and evidence was heard that the mines were primed by untrained personnel, whether these individuals were sailors of the British Navy or from the dockyard workers wasn't made clear. A faulty primer was blamed for the explosion which, in the circumstances, wasn't a total surprise as the primers used at the time were spring-loaded and known to be unstable, but still they were used, although in fairness to the authorities they were in the process of developing a safer version, albeit too late for those killed on the *Princess Irene*.

There were, as might be expected during a time of war, suspicions and suggestions that the explosion was down to an act of sabotage, but no proof or evidence to substantiate this theory was ever discovered.

The names of those who perished are commemorated on the Naval War Memorial at Southsea, at the Woodlands Road Cemetery in Gillingham, and at the dockyard church in Sheerness. The reason for the use of the Gillingham Cemetery was that the Admiralty had

1915 – DEEPENING CONFLICT

reserved a large section because of its proximity to the nearby Royal Naval Hospital in Windmill Road Gillingham.

A search of the Commonwealth War Graves website shows only seventeen separate graves from those who lost their lives on the *Princess Irene*:

Samuel George Castle	Stoker 2nd Class
Bertie Clarey	Hired Skilled Labourer
Philip William Turner Files	Signalman
Harry Goodger	Writer 1st Class
Ernest William Brown	Leading Stoker
William Charles James	Stoker 1st Class
Albert George Knieriem	Stoker 1st Class
Robert McQueen	Fireman
George Patrick Marshall	Stoker 2nd Class
William Robert Preston	Royal Marine Light Infantry
William Albert Snoop	Leading Seaman
Frederick James Timms	Ordinary Signalman
James Williamson	Royal Marine Light Infantry
Albert Willingham	Leading Stoker
John Donoghue	Mercantile Marine Reserve
Peter Galea	Officers Steward 3rd Class
Alexander William Arthur Daisley	Leading Signalman

Here is a list of the civilian dock workers who were killed with the explosion and sinking of the HMS *Princess Irene*:

Adams, F	Ackhurst, A	Back, H	Barling, N T
Barton, A	Bidgood, W T T	Blee, J	Branchett, E
Brazil, F	Bridges, S	Brown, F	Brown, H
Brown, J	Buckhurst, J	Burgess, A	Burrows, R
Callahan, E E	Cheeseman, H	Chittick, H	Clarey, B
Clay, C H	Collingbourne, J	Daniels, J	Dawe, C
Deal, J	English, G	Faxley, H	Fisher, C
Gamblin, W	Grout, A H	Grant, J G	Girvan, D

Goulding, J	Harris, B	Harrison, W	Hawkins, B
Howell, R	Irons, R	Jenner, R	Keeble, V
Keen, W	Kimber, E	Lawrence, H C	Lott, F C
Lupton, J	Mills, J R	Newman, A J	Noakes, F
Noakes, H	O'Callaghan, J	Pack, J	Potter, V
Proom, T	Pryke, S	Quicke, H	Rixon, J L
Rowswell, J	Rogers, J	Rogers, J	Slade, G
Spears, A S	Smith, W	Snelling, H	Stead, T J
Stephens, J	Stirling, R	Strevens, H	Stride, J
Susans, W	Trowell, E T	Turner, G	Watts, G T
Wigley, J	Wiseman, A	Wood, M	Wood, R
Young, P			

On 31 May 1915 there was an inquest into the deaths of two other victims of the explosion of HMS *Princess Irene*. They lived on the Isle of Grain, just across from Sheerness, at the mouth of the River Medway.

In relation to 47-year-old George Alfred Bradley, it was deemed that he died as a result of a heart attack, due to the shock he was caused on hearing the sound of the vessel exploding. George had five sons who served in the war. The Eldest was William, followed by Alexander who was a private (L/9300 and L/11639) in the 2nd Battalion, East Kent Regiment, George, Bert who was a private (H/33078 and L/20623) in the 14th Hussars (King's), Corps of Lancers, and Ambrose who initially served as a private (G/6276) in the East Kent Regiment before transferring to the Army Service Corps where he became a driver (ET/49271). There was a sixth son, Albert, who was born in 1901 and was too young to have served.

The other victim was 9-year-old Ida Barden. She was playing in the garden at her auntie's house on the Isle of Grain when a piece of metal from the *Princess Irene* hit her on the head and killed her. Mrs Doust, her auntie, had her hands on Ida's shoulders as she was hit.

On Friday, 20 August 1915, the Military Pass which had been in force on the Isle of Sheppey for the previous four months was replaced, making it the third type since they were first issued in November 1914. Any decision to change the passes was taken by the military authorities and was normally undertaken for security reasons. The longer a particular pass was in use the easier it would be for a forged copy to be used for clandestine purposes. By changing them on a regular, but unknown basis, there was less chance of them being utilised by the enemy.

The new passes for visitors to the Isle of Sheppey were obtainable from Sittingbourne police station. Those who travelled by rail and who wished to enter parts of the island that were outside the military canal at Sheerness could only obtain their passes from the Mayor of Queenborough. No pass was required to enter or leave Sheerness by anybody travelling by rail, but this did not apply to those who entered the Isle of Sheppey on the 'Kings Highway', via the Swale Bridge.

During the first ten months of their use, there had been only one serious misuse of the passes, which was not for spying purposes or on behalf of the enemy. On Friday, 5 August 1915, at the insistence of the commissioner of police, William Edward Bull of Walworth was summoned to Lambeth Police Court to answer the complaint of allowing his son, George Joseph Bull, to have possession of his travelling pass for the Isle of Sheppey. Mr Knights, prosecuting, informed the court that on 21 May 1915 the defendant obtained a pass for the purpose of his business as a traveller and also for the purpose of visiting his son, who lived in Sheerness.

On 6 and 7 July, a man named Gunnbridge, who was on a visit to the Isle of Sheppey, spoke to one of the coastguards in such a way as to arouse suspicion. The coastguard reported the matter to the military authorities with the result that on 9 July Lieutenant Gidney saw Gunnbridge, stopped him, and asked for his pass. He then produced the pass that belonged to William Edward Bull. Inquiries were made and it was found that the pass had been lent to Gunnbridge by George Bull, who had obtained it from his father. Both Gunnbridge and George Bull were arrested for using the pass contrary to regulations, placed before the Sittingbourne Petty Sessions, and on conviction were each fined £10.

Mr Stonehouse, defending William Edward Bull, told the court that his client had never had any intention of doing anything that could pose a threat to national security. He had already lost one son who had been killed in the war. Another was interned in Holland, while a third son was serving in the Royal Navy. Mr Chester Jones, chairman of the bench, told Mr Bull that although he had every sympathy with him in relation to his loss, he still had no option but to find him guilty of the charge and impose a fine of £20, because of the seriousness of the offence.

William Edward Bull had nine children, five sons and four daughters. Arthur Edward, the youngest of his sons, was killed in action on 9 May 1915 while serving on the Western Front in France. Even though he was only 18 years of age at the time of his death, he was a sergeant (1702) in the 21st Battalion (First Surrey Rifles) London Regiment. He is buried at the Guards Cemetery at Windy Corner in the village of Cuinchy in the Pas-de-Calais.

As for George, the 1911 census shows him as being a bedstead manufacturer's agent, but he clearly went on to greater things, as his will shows that when he died on 20 July 1960, aged 75 at King's College Hospital in London, he left a total of £105,973 3s 2d (worth £10 million today).

The story of a soldier's romance with a girl from the Isle of Sheppey, which saw him standing before a court in London facing a charge of obtaining money by false pretences, made the national press. On Friday, 27 August 1915, George Thomas Cox, a 26-year-old sergeant in the 5th Battalion, Rifle Brigade, was indicted at the London Sessions for obtaining £6 18s from Alfred Dye of Kentish Town. Cox, who was stationed on the Isle of Sheppey with his battalion, met the Mr Dye's daughter on the island. They later travelled to London and Cox went to live with her at her parent's house at 18 Leverton Street in Kentish Town. After a few weeks, Cox asked Alfred Dye if he could become engaged to his daughter. Mr Dye agreed and asked what prospects Cox had, to which he replied he had savings of £875 which was currently held in an account with the Bengal and Calcutta Bank but that he was in the process of having it transferred to a London Bank. Believing that his future son-in-law was solvent, Mr Dye lent him money on several occasions.

The banns for the marriage of Mr Cox and Miss Dye were published and the date of the wedding was set for 24 July 1915, but Cox failed to turn up and the couple were never married. Mr Dye had subsequently discovered that Cox's story about having such a large sum of money was a fabrication.

When giving evidence to the court, Cox said that he had made a fool of himself. He admitted that he had never had such a sum of money in any bank account, but that he had only ever borrowed a total of four pounds from Mr Dye. He said that in making the false statement to Mr Dye concerning his financial position he had no fraudulent intention and that he had always intended to repay the money.

Evidence was given to the court that showed Cox to have had an excellent character in the army and that he had not been the same man since his brother had been killed at Neuve Chapelle. Mr Cox had himself served in both India and France from where he was sent back to England suffering from frost bite. He had since been serving as a musketry instructor.

Having heard all of the evidence, the jury returned a verdict of 'not guilty'. In discharging Cox, the judge, Mr Lawrie, said that he entirely agreed with the verdict. Cox went back to his unit on the Isle of Sheppey where he continued serving as a musketry instructor.

Mr Alfred Dye had four daughters all of whom in 1915 would have all been old enough to date Mr Cox. They were Annie, Rebecca and Alice, who all worked as tailoresses, and Ruth who was a mother's help. I have not been able establish for sure which of the daughters it was who was due to become Cox's wife.

There was mention made during the court case of George's brother who had been killed at Neuve Chapelle. The Battle of Neuve Chapelle took place between 10 and 13 March 1915. A check of the Commonwealth War Graves Commission website shows that a total of eight men with the surname Cox were killed or died between those two dates. Six of these men have no known grave and are commemorated on the Le Touret Memorial, which is the memorial which includes the names of most of the men who fell during the battle of Neuve Chapelle and whose bodies were never recovered.

In early September 1915, while excavations at Minster on the Isle of Sheppey were underway, evidence of the island's past history unexpectedly came to light, in the shape of a well preserved Roman coin. It was sent to the British Museum in London for authentication and was confirmed to be a coin from the rule of Hadrian, whose reign lasted from AD 117 to 138. During the same excavations, other coins from more recent times were also discovered. This excavation was somewhat unusual as it contained coins from different reigns including Henry lll (1207-72), Edward l (1239-1307), Edward IV (1442-83), Henry Vll (1457-1509), Edward Vl (1537-53), and James Vl (1566-1625).

On 16 September 1915 local newspapers carried the news of the death of 71-year-old Mrs Mary Jane Copland. She was the wife of Mr John Copland, who had been for nearly forty years clerk to the Sheppey Board of Guardians, and for seven years the chairman of the Sheerness Urban District Council. The family lived at 3 Banks Terrace, Sheerness. Mrs Copland was well known and highly respected throughout the Isle of Sheppey. She was the second daughter of Mr Robert Palmer of Parsonage Farm, Minster, and married John Copland in 1868 when he was one of the island's up-and-coming young solicitors. Mrs Copland took a keen interest in philanthropic work and at the time of her death was a ruling councillor of the Sheerness Habitation of the Primrose League, which was an organisation for spreading Conservative principles throughout Great Britain.

The couple went on to have nine children, seven of whom were still alive at the time of Mary's death, three sons and four daughters: Mr Charles Palmer Copland, who was a well-known local cricketer

1915 – DEEPENING CONFLICT 51

in his younger years in Sheppey, had by 1915 emigrated to Australia and become a successful squatter, holding extensive areas of land in the state of Queensland. Mr William Shrubsole Copland was in charge of a post within the Arctic Circle; and Mr Henry Townsend Copland was the clerk of the Sheppey Board of Guardians and in partnership as a solicitor with his father. The four daughters were: Miss Mary Copland, who was the honorary secretary of the Lethbridge Sick Nursing Society; Mrs Campion, wife of Mr J.H.F. Campion, who had previously held the position of fleet paymaster; Mrs Row, wife of the then fleet paymaster, Mr P.H.L. Row; and the youngest of the sisters, Miss S. Copland.

Primrose League Badge.

An inquest at Sheerness was held on Thursday, 14 October 1915, to look in to the deaths of two soldiers who were killed during a training accident on the island on 11 October that saw four other men injured. Remarkably, no evidence was provided by the military authorities to explain how the explosion was caused, although it was unarguably the result of an exploding grenade. Despite the omission of this vital explanation, the jury somehow managed to return a verdict of 'accidental death', which, although it was most probably how the deaths of the soldiers occurred, hardly seems an adequate explanation.

The jury also made the suggestion that further such accidents should be avoided, without providing any sensible suggestions as to how that could best be achieved.

The two soldiers killed in the incident were Vincent Walker, a 20-year-old rifleman (S/10950) with the 6th Battalion, Rifle Brigade. His family were from Plumstead and he is buried in the town's local cemetery. The other man was George Henry Johnson, a 21-year-old rifleman (S/10995), who was also serving with the 6th Battalion, Rifle Brigade. His family were from Uxbridge and he is buried at the Hillingdon and Uxbridge Cemetery. The four injured men were Corporal Vaughan, who was one of the training staff, and Riflemen Ball, Dumbavin and Jenkins, all of whom were members of the 6th Battalion, Rifle Brigade.

As best could be ascertained, the grenade exploded while it was being held by Rifleman Walker, the suggestion being that it was faulty in some way, which, if it was the case, was indeed a tragic accident.

On Saturday, 13 November 1915, an article appeared in the *Western Mail* about a photograph of a young woman which had been found by Lance Corporal F. Dennis of the 1st Battalion, Rifle Brigade, on the Western Front in Belgium. It was in a letter addressed to Sergeant (1172) Davies, 2nd Battalion, Monmouthshire Regiment. There was no return address on the letter and the article in the newspaper was an attempt to try to locate relatives of the sergeant so that the letter and photograph could be returned to them. One can only assume that Sergeant Davies had handed the letter to the lance corporal and asked him to return it to his family. Lance Corporal Dennis was with Sergeant Davies when he was initially wounded and remained with him until he passed away a short while later on 26 May. On his return to the United Kingdom, Lance Corporal Dennis returned to his barracks with the Rifle Brigade at Leysdown. It was fortunate that Lance Corporal Dennis took the letter because in the heat of battle Sergeant Davies's body was lost and once the fighting had stopped it could not be found. Davies has no known grave and his name is commemorated on the Ypres (Menin Gate) Memorial. A check of the Commonwealth War Graves Commission website shows that there was a Corporal (3925) Frank Dennis of the 2nd Battalion, Rifle Brigade, who was killed in action on 29 March 1917 and who is buried at the New British Cemetery in Gouzeaucourt, which is situated in the Nord region of France. I have no way of knowing with any degree of certainty if this is the same person.

The Folkestone coroner held an inquest in relation to the death of John Henry Blake who died on Monday, 6 December 1915. Blake was a private (T/4315) in the 4th Battalion, The Buffs (East Kent Regiment), and was stationed at Canterbury. He was found dead from a gunshot wound in the home of his brother-in-law at 16 Sidney Street, Folkestone. He was 40 years of age and had only enlisted a few weeks before his death. He had told his brother-in-law that he had been practically forced to join the army, a situation that he was very agitated about as he had what he described as a crippled back, in the form of a 'big lump coming out like a camel every time he stooped', an ailment which he was sure would prevent him from enlisting, but much to his surprise he was accepted. He had said that the lump was so pronounced that he couldn't properly put all of his equipment on. His sergeant had told him to go and see the doctor again, and when he did the doctor simply told him to carry on. He was due back at his barracks in Canterbury at 0930 hours on Monday, 6 December 1915, but at that exact same hour he was found dead in the kitchen of his brother-in-law's house. He had a bullet wound to his chest and an army rifle was lying at the side of his body. The jury returned a verdict of suicide while temporarily insane.

John Henry Blake was originally from Iwade. The 1911 census showed that the occupants of 16 Sidney Street, Folkestone, were Mrs Florence Ellen May, her 5-year-old son John Richard May, and her brother Edmund Finn Burvill who had been in the Royal Navy between 6 July 1903 and 8 April 1909. It is probable that by the time of John Henry Blake's death the occupants of 16 Sidney Street had changed.

CHAPTER 4

1916
The Realisation

❖

1916 was to be another busy year. It began on 1 January with the Royal Army Medical Corps carrying out the first blood transfusion using stored blood that had been cooled.

With the fighting at Gallipoli not having gone well, the last of the British and Australian forces were evacuated from the peninsula on 9 January.

The implementation of the Military Services Act 1916 brought in conscription when it was passed into law on 27 January and became effective from 2 March. This in effect put Britain on a total war footing, sending out a clear message to Germany and her allies that Britain only had one intention and that was to win the war outright, no matter what the cost in money or lives.

The Military Medal, for men from 'other ranks,' was instituted as a military decoration on 25 March.

The Battle of Jutland was the only large-scale meeting of battleships of the war, as the British Grand Fleet with its armada of 151 ships took on the 99 ships of the German High Seas Fleet. It lasted for two days, 31 May and 1 June. It was arguable who won the encounter, with Britain losing 14 of her ships and the Germans losing 9.

Lord Kitchener, who had played such an important part in the early part of the war, was killed on 5 June when the vessel he was on, HMS *Hampshire*, was hit by a mine and sank off the Isle of Orkney.

The Battle of the Somme began with the blast of a whistle on 1 July, in what turned out to be one of the bloodiest battles of the war. On the first day alone, there were 57,470 British and Commonwealth casualties. General Haig appeared unmoved by such heavy losses. By the end of the battle, 4½ months later, that number has risen to 420,000.

On 2 September, Lieutenant William Leefe Robinson of the Royal Flying Corps became the first pilot to shoot down a German airship over Britain.

The 7 September saw the Isle of Sheppey designated as a Special Military Area, which greatly restricted access to people who didn't live there.

There was a change of Prime Minister as Asquith resigned and David Lloyd George succeeded him on 7 December.

And towards the end of the year, Germany offered to enter into peace negotiations with Britain and her allies. The mediator for these negotiations was the President of the United States, Woodrow Wilson. Britain didn't want a negotiated peace settlement, they wanted to comprehensively beat the Germans to make sure that she did not rear her ugly head again any time soon. There was a strongly held belief that after the losses they had sustained during the battles of the Somme and Verdun, Germany had had enough of the war and wanted an end to it.

A check on the Commonwealth War Graves Commission website for those men from the Isle of Sheppey who were killed or died during the Battle of the Somme brings up just one man. For a complete list of those from the island who were killed, I also had to search under the town names of Leysdown, Sheerness, Blue Town, Marine Town, Sheppey, Minster, Eastchurch and Queenborough. But even this is not a guarantee that I have managed to collect all the names from the Isle of Sheppey who fell during the Battle of the Somme.

James Shrubsole was one of those who fought and died during the Battle of the Somme. He was born in 1887 in Eastchurch on the Isle of Sheppey and was a labourer before he enlisted on 3 August 1915 at Canterbury, becoming a private (G/8144) in the 6th Battalion, The Buffs (East Kent Regiment). Even though he was nearly 29 years of age when he enlisted, I can only assume that he either very quickly became homesick or regretted his decision to enlist, as after only three days of being a soldier he went absent without leave. He was eventually detained by the civil police in Milton Regis on 16 August 1915 and returned to his battalion. As a punishment for his offence he was confined to barracks for seven days and docked five days' pay. Arriving in France on 23 December 1915 as part of the British Expeditionary Force, Shrubsole was wounded during fighting on 3 July 1916 and although he was treated at the 36th Field Ambulance, he died later the same day, the third day of the Battle of the Somme. He is buried at Millencourt Communal Cemetery Extension in the Somme region. According to the Commonwealth War Graves Commission website, James's parents, Mr and Mrs John Shrubsole, lived at Little Brooks House, Leysdown, but on his army service record, John and Annie Shrubsole were shown as living at Rayam Farm, Eastchurch. A letter from John Shrubsole to his son's regiment dated 24 November 1916, confirming receipt of his personal effects, shows that the family were living at Little Brooks House, Leysdown. James had already left home by the time he had enlisted and his home address was shown as 75 Hythe Road, Milton Regis. He was one of seven children, with a brother, Sidney, who had been too young to serve during the war, and five sisters.

During the Battle of Albert, which took place between 1 and 13 July 1916, Fourth Army's objectives were to take Montauban, Mametz, Fricourt, Contalmaison, and La Boisselle. They were successful in achieving all of their objectives. I found the names of thirteen men who had a connection with Sheerness who fell in the Battle of Albert (the 6th Battalion, The Buffs, along with the 6th

Battalion, Queen's Own (Royal West Kent Regiment), the 6th Battalion, The Queens (Royal West Surrey Regiment), the 7th Battalion, East Surrey Regiment, the 37th Machine Gun Company, the 37th Trench Mortar Battery and the 5th Battalion, Northamptonshire Regiment, made up the 37th Brigade. Along with the 35th and 36th Brigade they made up the 12th Eastern Division, which in turn were part of the lll Corps, which in turn were part of the Fourth Army).

Henry Ernest Conroy was born in Sheerness in 1893, the youngest child and only son of John and Lavinia Conroy, who lived at 3 Alma Street, Sheerness. Before the war he worked with his father, who was a skilled labourer, and his brother, a stoker, at HM Dockyard in Sheerness, as a messenger, while his sister Margaret worked locally in domestic service. During the war he originally enlisted in the East Kent Regiment as Private 9123 before later transferring to the 7th Battalion, The Queen's (Royal West Surrey Regiment) as Private G/24717. He was killed in action on the final day of the Battle of the Somme and is buried at the Grandcourt Road Cemetery, in the village of Grandcourt, which is situated about six miles north of the town of Albert.

The war diaries for the 7th Battalion, The Queens (Royal West Surrey Regiment) are sparse, but they show that the battalion moved in to hutments near Ovillers, and at zero hour (6.10 am) on 18 November 1916, two of the battalion's companies carried out an attack on the German-held Desire Trench. The morning of 18 November was extremely cold, with both snow and rain falling in quick succession, making the ground very slippery. There was little light at the start of the attack, making the conditions similar to that of a night attack. Having covered some 200 yards in distance and still with a further 100 yards to go until they reached Desire trench, the attacking companies came under heavy German rifle and machine gun fire from both flanks which resulted in heavy casualties. It is likely that it was during this attack that Henry was killed.

The above information was taken from a report of the actions of 18 and 19 November 1916 written by the battalion's commanding officer, Lieutenant Colonel M. Kemp-Welch. It contained the following paragraph which might appear somewhat surprising:

> *From survivors of 'C' and 'D' Companies, the following information has been obtained. Survivors have proved to be far from the best men of the Companies and their statements are accepted with reserve.*

Alexander Macdonald was born in Sheerness in 1898 and enlisted in the army soon after his eighteenth birthday, when he became a gunner (69652) in the 52nd Battery, Royal Field Artillery. He was killed in action on 9 August 1916, still 18 years of age, and is buried at the Dernancourt Communal Cemetery Extension, Dernancourt being a village about a mile and a half south of Albert. It was also the location of the main dressing station for the XV Corps, as well as a Field Ambulance unit. The family home was at 6 Marjorie Terrace, Sheerness. Evan and Pricilla Macdonald had four other children besides Alexander: Edmund, Kennedy and Roy, and their only daughter, Georgina.

William M.J. Vaughan was a sergeant (13214) in the 3rd Battalion, Grenadier Guards. He had first arrived in France on 26 July 1915 and after initially having been reported as missing in action on 14 September 1916, he was subsequently recorded as having been killed in action sometime between 14 and 17 September 1916. It was at this time that the Guards Division attacked the German defensive positions at Lesboeufs, which they eventually captured on 25 September. Vaughan was 28 years of age at the time of his death and his final resting place was at the Guards Cemetery in the village of Lesboeufs. Although he was a native of Sheerness, his parents, William and Mary Ann, lived at 37 Nelson Road, Whitstable, Kent.

E.A. Deadman was a private (L/10488) in the 6th Battalion, The Buffs, (East Kent Regiment), when he was killed in action on

7 October 1916. He is buried at the Bancourt British Cemetery. By the time the Commonwealth War Graves Commission had started compiling their records, Private Deadman's mother had remarried and was Mrs F.A. Lane of 51 Chapel Street, Blue Town, Sheerness.

George Arthur Packer was 20 years of age and a private (L/10453) in the 6th Battalion, The Buffs, (East Kent Regiment) when he was killed in action on 7 October 1916, yet only a year earlier he had been minding his own business as a labourer. He enlisted on 13 May 1915 at Sheerness, not quite 19 years of age. The harsh realities of military life quickly became apparent to him when he was confined to barracks for two days, punishment for committing the heinous offence of having a light on his barracks room at 10.30 pm. Initially he had been reported as missing in action; his death was then presumed to have taken place on the same day that he had been reported missing. His body was never recovered and his name is commemorated on the Thiepval Memorial. His army service record showed his mother, Mary Ann Packer, of 2 School Lane, New Town, Sheerness, as his next of kin. The same document also shows the family as having lived at 30 Chapel Street, Blue Town, Sheerness. It also showed him as having six brothers and four sisters. George had cause to visit number 12 Rest Station on 10 February 1916 suffering with influenza; he remained there only for a day before returning to his battalion. On 20 March 1916, George was sent back to England suffering with trench foot. He was admitted to the Royal Victoria Hospital at Netley where he remained for the next two months before returning to France on 23 May 1916. During his period of time back in England he was given a furlough from 2 to 11 May 1916 so that he could spend time with his family. Little did George or any of his family realise that this would be the last time that they would see each other.

George's younger brother Charles, had enlisted in the army before the end of the war and was with the Rifle Brigade. Both the 5th and 6th Reserve battalions, which had originally been stationed at Winchester, but on mobilisation at the beginning of the war, the 5th Battalion moved to Minster on the Isle of Sheppey, where it remained throughout the war as part of the Thames and Medway Garrison. The 6th Battalion initially moved to Sheerness and then in March 1916 it moved across the island to Eastchurch, where it also became part of the Thames and Medway Garrison. Both battalions became Depot and Training units.

Frederick J. Bailey was the son of William and Mary Ann Bailey of 'Antrim', The Glen, Minster. He enlisted during the war into the 1st/6th Battalion, London Regiment (City of London). He was promoted to the rank of lance corporal (3218) and was killed in action on 22 October 1916 when he was 24 years of age. His body was never recovered and he has no known grave, so, as was the way, his name is recorded on the Ypres (Menin Gate) Memorial. Before the war he was a gas fitter's labourer, but like a lot of young men of his generation, when his country needed him, he enlisted out of choice and went off to fight. So did his younger brother, Ernest, who had been an office boy in a firm of solicitors before the war. Like Frederick, he served with the 1st/6th Battalion, London Regiment (City of London), and, like Frederick, he was one of the war's victims, killed on the very same day as his brother, possibly side by side when they died. Imagine how William and Mary Ann Bailey felt when not only did they lose two of their sons in the war, but on the very same day in the very same action.

The war diaries of the 1st/6th Battalion, London Regiment (City of London), for 22 October 1918 partly read as follows:

Battalion in the trenches at 6am, while 'Standing To' the Germans exploded 2, possibly 3 mines underneath C & D companies and to the north of D company.

As if the detonation of the three mines wasn't bad enough, the Germans followed this with a heavy artillery bombardment of the British positions. Besides those who were killed and wounded as a result of the explosions, more casualties were incurred by the British when those men who had been tasked with trying to dig out their entombed colleagues came under attack from rapidly advancing German forces, with grenades, rifle and machine gun fire. There was even a period during the fighting that artillery shells and trench mortars fired by the British sadly landed in their own trenches, causing both casualties and considerable damage.

Taking in to account the carnage and devastation that was caused by the detonation of the mines and the subsequent artillery bombardment by the Germans, it was remarkable that the British sustained such relatively few casualties. Four officers were wounded, two other ranks were killed, with fifty other ranks being wounded and three more reported as missing. The entries in a battalion's war diary usually consisted of a couple of lines at most. In this case, so sudden, unexpected, and intense was the fighting, that the written report of the action took more than five pages to do it justice.

George Ernest James Norman was 22 years of age and a Bombardier (38482) in 'D' Battery, 83rd Brigade, Royal Field Artillery, first arriving in France on 25 July 1915. He didn't die of his wounds, neither was he killed in action, instead he died of meningitis on 14 November 1916. He is buried in the Communal Cemetery in the village of Hem which is situated in the Somme region, on the south of the River Authie. Between September 1916 and February 1917, the 2/1st South Midland Casualty Clearing Station were located in the village, which was the reason for the location of the cemetery. According to the Commonwealth War Graves Commission website, George's parents, George and Mary Ann Eunice Norman, lived at Furzefield Cottages, Warden Road, Eastchurch, Isle of Sheppey. I then found an entry in the 1911 census which showed a George and Mary Ann Norman living at the same address in Eastchurch as had been recorded on the Commonwealth War Graves Commission website, which provided me with some certainty that I had found the same family. The same census showed that George and Mary had been married for twenty-four years, a marriage which had seen them blessed with six children, although one of them died before 1911. Both the 1901 and 1911 censuses showed the same five children – Emmie, Ethel, Ernest, Thomas and William – with George and Mary having married some time in 1887. I can only assume that their sixth child was born and died sometime between 1897 and 31 March 1901. As can be seen by the list of names of their children, none of them had the name of George Ernest James Norman. Although I am happy that I have the correct family for George, I can offer no rational explanation for the obvious ambiguity.

Robert Attew was a rifleman (P/913) in 'A' Company, 16th (Service) Battalion (St Pancras), Rifle Brigade, who had first arrived in France on 8 March 1916. Five weeks later, and even though it was the height of spring, he was suffering with influenza, his condition being sufficiently bad that he had to be treated by the 132nd Field Ambulance Unit. He was killed in action six months later on 3 September 1916. At the time of his death he was 34 years of age and he is buried at the Hamel Military Cemetery in the small French village Beaumont-Hamel. Two days before departing these shores he wrote his last will and testament, in which he left all his worldly goods to his wife. His widow, Emily Attew, lived at 1 North Street, Mile Town, Sheerness, with their son, Victor Maurice, who at the time of Robert's death was 7 years of age. Robert and Emily had married on 20 May 1907 at Christ Church, St Pancras in London. At the time of Robert's enlistment on 25 May 1915, the couple were living at 73 Stanhope Street, St Pancras. Emily received a pension from the Army's Ministry of Pensions Department, for her and their son Victor. It began on 26 March 1917, when the weekly payments were 17/6 and a week later it increased to 18/9.

Henry Westbrook was a sergeant (86) in the 6th Battery, 40 Brigade of the Royal Field Artillery. Having arrived in France on 19 August 1914, he died of his wounds at No. 21 Casualty Clearing Station on 19 July 1916 which at the time was in the village of La Neuville. He is buried at the La Neuville British Cemetery, Corbie.

He lived with his wife Catherine at 5 Newcomen Road, Sheerness. They had married on the island in August 1908.

Henry's best man at his wedding was Joseph Brown, who in 1911 was living at 5 Marine Parade, Sheerness, but by 1915 had moved on to 42 Alexander Road. Henry's son, Archibald John Brown, had enlisted at Sheerness on 2 November 1915, and became Private 702757 in the 23rd Battalion, London Regiment. He served in France for three months between 29 June and 28 September 1916 when he was wounded in action and returned to England suffering with a gunshot wound to his right arm. Although his army service record didn't go into the details of his injury, it must have been fairly serious as he was discharged from the army for no longer being physically fit and saw no further active service. As was in keeping with the times, Archibald was awarded his personalised numbered (417756) war badge, which was issued to men who had served in the armed services and because of injury or illness were no longer able to do so. The war badge identified its owner as having served his country and done his duty. This helped prevent the wearer from being thought of as a coward or from being verbally abused in the streets. The issue of such a badge to an individual was a one-off and would not be reissued under any circumstances.

Edward Sole was 33 years of age and a rifleman (3584) in the 2nd Battalion, King's Royal Rifle Corps, when he died of his wounds on 15 July 1916. He is buried at the Heilly Station Cemetery in the village of Méricourt-l'Abbé in the Somme. Before the war he lived with his parents at 52 Clyde Street, Sheerness, and worked as a labourer in HM Dockyard there. He had two elder brothers. The eldest, Harry, was three years older than him, born in 1879, and Albert, a year older, born in 1881. I could not discover for certain whether either of Edward's brothers served during the war, although according to the British army's medal rolls index for the same period, there were men with both the names Harry and Albert Sole who did. If they did serve, then they both survived.

James Henry Sugg was 39 years of age and an acting corporal (SR-7311–282311) in the 126th Siege Battery, Royal Garrison

Artillery when he was killed in action on 3 October 1916. He is buried at the Bernafay Wood British Cemetery in the village of Montauban, which is one of the numerous cemeteries in the Somme region. He was a married man and before going off to war was a labourer. He lived with his wife Alice Ivy at 77 Rose Street, Mile Town, Sheerness. At the time of the 1911 census, they were living at 18 Short Street, Mile Town, and had two young children, Arthur, the eldest by six years, and a daughter, Winifred.

David Stone was 32 years of age and, having enlisted at Margate, became a private (G/8782) in the 6th Battalion, The Buffs, (East Kent Regiment). He was killed in action on 7 October 1916 and is buried in the British Cemetery in the village of Bancourt. As the cemetery wasn't begun until September 1918, David must have initially been buried elsewhere and moved to Bancourt after the Armistice. The most likely location would, I suggest, be what was known as the Cloudy Trench Cemetery at Gueudecourt, where forty British soldiers who died between October and November 1916 were buried. His parents lived in Sheerness.

A check on the town of Eastchurch threw up one name of a soldier who had died at the Somme. Thomas Rogers was just 20 years of age and a private (G/8896) in the 10th (Kent County) Battalion, Queen's Own (Royal West Kent Regiment), when he was killed in action on 9 October 1916 during fighting at the Battle of the Transloy Ridges, which was one of the encounters which made up the Battle of the Somme. The battalion was raised in Maidstone a year earlier and, having completed their basic training at Aldershot, arrived in France on 4 May 1916. Thomas has no known grave and his name is recorded on and commemorated by its inclusion on the Thiepval Memorial. For me, Thomas was somewhat unique in that he was the foster son of Mrs Harriet Price, who lived at 1 Halls Cottages, Lower Road, Eastchurch. The uniqueness came in the shape of him being the first person I had discovered in all of my research who had been a foster child.

Throughout the nineteenth century there had been different forms of fostering, but the first actual laws in relation to it hadn't come in to place until 1926. It was undoubtedly the First World War which greatly helped expedite the situation, with more and more adoption societies and child rescue organisations springing up all over the place to cope with the big increase in children who found themselves being given up for adoption. Prior to this all that such a child would have had to look forward to would have been an upbringing in an orphanage or the workhouse.

A check on Queenborough threw up five more names of soldiers who died at the Somme. Lionel Arthur Bartlett was 30 years of age and a lieutenant in 1st Battalion, Queen's Own (Royal West Kent Regiment). He arrived in France in May 1916 and on 22 July was killed in action. He is buried in the Pozières British Cemetery, Ovillers-la-Boisselle. At the time of his death his widow, Jessie Emma Bartlett, was living at 46 Fairfield Road, Bromley, Kent. His father, Ernest William Bartlett, had previously been the Vicar of Queenborough.

Arthur Albert Robson was born on 11 March 1896 in Queenborough on the Isle of Sheppey and before the war he worked as a 'glass gatherer'. He was 20 years of age and a lance corporal (L/10604) in 'B' Company, 1st Battalion, Queen's Own (Royal West Kent Regiment), when he was killed on 22 July 1916. He was buried at the Caterpillar Valley Cemetery in the village of Longueval. At the time of Arthur's death there had been some extremely heavy fighting in the area, as British forces did their best to wrestle the village out of the control of the Germans. His parents, William and Mary, lived at 26 Castle Street, Queenborough. They had been blessed with twelve children over the years, although by the time of the 1911 census, two of them were shown as already having died. Arthur had enlisted on 8 December 1914 at Sheerness. What was interesting about his attestation form was that it was for seven years with the colours and five years in the Army Reserve and not for the duration of the war. Maybe at the time nobody was expecting that the war was going to last very long. Thankfully it didn't end up lasting for twelve years. Arthur's army service record shows that he was initially listed as missing in action, but on the same page it also gave the location of his burial:

Buried: Caterpillar Valley Cemetery just west of Longueval, six and a half miles east north east of Albert. Report by Graves Registration and Exhumations Unit.

Although Arthur's body was recovered for burial, its initial discovery couldn't have been immediate as there was an additional entry added under the comments about the location of his burial:

Killed in action or died of his wounds on or shortly after 22 July 1916. Expeditionary Force France.

Such was the confusion surrounding Arthur's death that six weeks after what was subsequently officially recorded as the date that he died, his family still did not know if he was alive or dead. His father William sent the following very brief letter to the Infantry Record Office at Hounslow. It was dated 12 September 1916:

Sir,
Could you kindly inform me, if any news or information, has been received of 10604 L/C Robson, A, R.W. Kents.
   Yours in anticipation
   Mr Robson.

What if any reply Arthur's father received, is not recorded on his army service record?

Arthur had five brothers, two older than him and three younger. Two were not old enough to have served in the military during the war. The only one who I could find as having definitely served during the war was Frederick, who enlisted in the Royal Navy two weeks after his eighteenth birthday, on 28 September 1918. Less than six months later, and with the war finally at an end, he was demobilised on 3 March 1919.

Harold Norman Ketley enlisted in the army on 14 March 1915 at Sheerness and at the time his home address was shown as being 3 Whiteway, Queenborough. Prior to enlisting he had been a labourer, nearly 5 feet 9 inches in height, and with tattoos on both arms. He was 28 years of age and a private (G/6000) in the 1st Battalion, The Buffs (East Kent Regiment), when he was killed in action during the fighting of the Battle of the Somme on 15 September 1916. The war diaries for the 1st Battalion, The Buffs, for this particular day, read in part as follows:

At 0620 am the artillery barrage opened and the battalion left the Assembly trenches. The signal was then given to change direction, half right and get in to assault formation. The battalion was then facing NE between points T21 C49 and T20 D49.

At 0635 am the battalion commenced to advance and at once came under heavy machine gun fire from point 141.7 and a large number of officers and men were hit. It was found that this point (141.7) had not been captured and that consequently it was impossible to advance to our objective.

This was more than likely the moment when Harold was killed. It is a strong possibility that he was one of those hit by machine gun fire as he left the safety of the trench. There were 128 officers and men from the 1st Battalion, The Buffs, who were killed that day. Harold is buried at the Guillemont Road Cemetery in the village of Guillemont. According to the 1911 census the family home was at 6 School Lane, Sheerness, but by the end of the war his parents John and Lucy and his elder sister Emily had moved to 97 High Street, Queenborough.

Ernest Henry Runham was the youngest of three children. His sister Elizabeth and brother William were eight and six years older than him respectively. After he left school, he become a grocer's assistant, but just before his twentieth birthday, on 9 April 1915, he enlisted in the army at Woolwich and became Bombardier 95370 in the artillery. After having completed his basic training at No.6 Training Depot in Glasgow, he was initially posted to the Artillery's Reserve Brigade, before being sent out to France on 20 November 1915. He was posted to 'A' Battery, 50th Brigade, Royal Field Artillery, on 8 December 1915, where he remained, except for a week's home leave between 9 and 16 June 1916, for the following ten months until he was killed in action, aged 21, on 26 October 1916. He is buried at the Bazentin-le-Petit Military Cemetery in the Somme. The cemetery was first used at the end of July 1916 after the village and surrounding areas had been captured from German forces. By the end of the war, Ernest's parents, George, who was a carpenter at HM Dockyard, Sheerness, and Laura, who was a maternity nurse for Kent Council, lived at Vernon Villa, High Street, Queenborough, although at the time of the 1911 census, they were living at 1 Castle Road in Queenborough. Ernest's brother William had been a train driver before the war, and although I discovered a William Dunham who served in both the Duke of Cambridge's Own (Middlesex Regiment) and the Labour Corps, I have no way of being able to determine if this is the same person. Either way, William survived the war, and on 27 April 1930, when he was 40 years old, he emigrated to Canada, arriving in Montreal, Quebec, having left Liverpool on board the SS *Laurentic* on 19 April.

Before the war Ernest Bentley was a skilled labourer. He was happily married to Una Maria Keen, both having been 20 years of age on their wedding day, 31 October 1908, at Sheerness Registry Office. A son, Ernest junior, arrived six months later, on 29 April 1909, when they were living at 21 Pottery Buildings, Johnsons Cottages, New Road, Queenborough, so Una was already pregnant at the time of the marriage. Two daughters would follow, Winifred, born on 22 July 1911, and Jessie, on 3 December 1913. Ernest enlisted in the army less than a month after the outbreak of war, on 2 September 1914, at Sheerness, joining the 6th Battalion, Queen's Own (Royal West Kent Regiment), and arriving in France the following year. On 12 March 1916 he was wounded in action when he received gunshot wounds to his left arm and leg. He was admitted to No.6 General Hospital in Rouen, before being transferred to one of the many hospitals at Étaples on 20 April. He was there for ten days before he was returned to his unit on 30 April. Two months later he was admitted to 1st South Midlands Casualty Clearing Station in France as a result of spraining an ankle. He was also seen by the nearby 38th Field Ambulance Unit for the same ailment. He was promoted to the rank of lance corporal on 28 April 1915 and further promoted to corporal on 3 July 1916, two days after the start of the Battle of the Somme. Ernest was wounded in action on 7 October 1916 and died of his wounds the next day. In September 1916 the XV Corps Main Dressing Station was established in the village, and this is more than likely where Ernest had his wounds treated before he died. He is buried at what is now called the Dartmoor Cemetery, in the village of Bécordel-Bécourt, a mile south-east of Albert. When the cemetery was begun in August 1915 it was known as the Bécordel-Bécourt Military Cemetery, but at the request of the 8th and 9th battalions, Devonshire Regiment, its name was changed in May 1916. After the war Ernest's widow Una was living at 21 Stanley Avenue, Queenborough. She had been awarded an army pension for her and her three children of 27/6 per week which began on 23 April 1917. But most likely this was stopped when she remarried, becoming Mrs William Hicks in August 1919. William was a local man from Leysdown.

On Tuesday, 15 February 1916, a man, whose name was not released by the authorities, and who was an electrical fitter employed by the Admiralty at HM Dockyards at Sheerness, applied before the Metropolitan Munitions Tribunal for his discharge. He did so on the grounds that, as overtime had been abolished, his wages were insufficient to provide for himself and the running costs of his home in Ashton-under-Lyne. He wanted to be allowed to return home so that he could find work in the Manchester area. He told the tribunal that there were six fitters, two labourers and an assistant doing the job which one man had done before the war, which was, he said, one of the main reasons why his overtime had been so greatly reduced.

In response, a representative from the Admiralty said that nobody who worked at the dockyards in Sheerness had ever been promised any overtime and that the man in question had worked almost continuous overtime between February 1915 and January 1916, which made his average weekly earnings £4 6s 3d. The Admiralty representative added that it was difficult to find electrical fitters, and with the country at war it was surely understandable to most people that there was a need to maintain a large dockyard workforce to deal with every eventuality that could befall at any time. It was not only important, but a necessity, to ensure that the nation had an efficient and fully operational fleet of ships able to protect the country from its enemies. The man was refused a certificate allowing him to stop working at Sheerness Dockyard.

Lieutenant Commander H.C. Stahl of the Royal Navy was killed not by enemy action, but a tragic accident. The adjourned inquest took place at Sheerness on 15 February 1916 in relation to the death of the Lieutenant Commander, who was in command of a small naval auxiliary vessel, HM Trawler *King Emperor*, on 4 February 1916 when it was in collision with the Swedish steamer *Kattegat*. Stahl died from injuries sustained in the collision as well as from exposure to the harsh elements that prevailed at the time. Ordinary Telegraphist Wilfred Buggy, who was only 18 years of age, told the inquest that the collision took place at 5.30 in the morning, and that when he was thrown into the sea as the two vessels collided, Commander Stahl grabbed him by his scarf and pulled him towards the fore rigging of the *King Emperor*, where they remained until they were both rescued about an hour and a half later. Commander Stahl passed away shortly after having been rescued. The collision happened just before dawn. At the time, Commander Stahl had been in his bunk, and was wearing only a shirt as he had not had time to fully dress. While waiting to be rescued, the commander had said to Buggy that he could not hold on any longer, so the young telegraphist gave him his scarf enabling Stahl to tie himself to the ship's rigging. Medical evidence suggested that he may well have sustained a fracture to his skull. At the time of the collision, the *King Emperor* was at anchor with none of her lights switched on. Although this was possibly for security reasons, it proved to be a fateful decision which cost Commander Stahl his life. The crew of the *Kattegat*, which was being navigated by a Trinity House pilot at the time of the accident, did not see the *King Emperor* until she struck her. The jury returned a verdict of accidental death and exonerated the pilot of the *Kattegat* from any blame for the collision. In the subsequent newspaper reports of the incident and the inquest, the *King Emperor* was not named but simply referred to as the 'auxiliary'.

On 26 February 1916, Mr Richard Cleeve, who had previously been the chief officer of HM Coastguard, was presented with a handsome walking stick and briar pipe by the crew of the HM Coastguard station at St Margaret's as a token of their respect on the occasion of his retirement. Chief Officer Cleeve had served for nearly forty years in the Royal Navy and Coastguard service and had been in charge of St Margaret's Coastguard Station since November 1911. During his years of service, he took part in the Zulu War of 1875 and the First Boer War of 1881 on board HMS *Boadicea*. His last position was at Sheerness, and it was while employed there on the examination service between July 1914 and November 1915 that, as a result of what was described as a 'severe breakdown', he was medically discharged from the service. He was 54 years of age and went on to a long and happy retirement, passing away in 1941 aged 79. He had married Mary Ann Shepperd in August 1886 and they had four children, sons Richard and Harold, and daughters Mary and Lilian. Richard enlisted in the Royal Army Service Corps on 4 December 1915 and, having survived the war, was finally demobilised on 17 October 1919.

On Friday, 24 March 1916, at the sitting of the Sheerness Rural Tribunal, which had recently come into being under the Military Services Act, the following relevant applications were made. Vernon

George Green, who was 35 years of age and a musician, made an application for absolute exemption from having to undertake military training, on the grounds of ill health and because he was a conscientious objector. What ailment he was suffering from was not explained. He claimed to be a direct descendent of William Penn, the Quaker and founder of Pennsylvania, and in his written appeal Green said, 'I was brought up under strict Christian principles not to take life in any form.' Having heard his application, the members of the Sheerness Rural Tribunal refused him an exemption from military service. Green was born in London in about 1883. His mother was Mary Ann Penn Horsefall and his father was Vernon senior. I was unable to establish whether or not Vernon ended up undertaking military service during the First World War, but if he did, he survived as he lived into his nineties.

At the same tribunal, Mr W.E. Charlton, who was the manager of the Sheerness and District Electric Power and Traction Company, applied for exemption certificates for one inspector and three motor bus drivers. Mr Charlton told the tribunal that some women had been trained up as drivers, but they could not stand the weather. Short term exemptions were given to two of the drivers, but the tribunal decided not to make any decision in relation to the inspector and the other driver as the group to which they belonged had not yet been called up for military service.

On a separate matter, the chairman of the tribunal, Mr C. Ingleton, made mention that it was becoming popular for young men who had previously worked as labourers on some of the local farms to seek new employment at Sheerness Dockyard or in nearby munitions factories in an apparent act to escape military service. Mr Ingleton said that he would make representation to the President of the Board of Agriculture on the matter.

An announcement was made at Sheerness dockyards by a high ranking official of the Admiralty on 1 April 1916 in relation to a Zeppelin raid on the east coast of England which resulted in the bringing down of Zeppelin *L15* in the Thames estuary off Kent. The crew of the Zeppelin were then rescued by the steam trawler

1916 – THE REALISATION   73

Olivine whose commander, Lieutenant W.R. Mackintosh, was a member of the Royal Naval Reserve. Having picked up the German prisoners, the crew of the *Olivine* handed them over to another vessel and continued with her duties. It appears that the crew of the trawler, who at the time were actively searching for the downed Zeppelin, first spotted them at about 3.30 am in calm seas. It was a dark night with a slight haze. The weather conditions were favourable for the Zeppelin's crew as their slowly sinking vessel was able to stay afloat long enough for them to be rescued from what could otherwise have been a watery grave. As soon as the *Olivine* was able to get close enough to the sinking Zeppelin, the Germans immediately indicated that they wished to surrender. There were a total of fifteen officers and men, although it was known that Zeppelin crews sometimes numbered as many as twenty-two or twenty-three on some of the biggest vessels. Even though Lieutenant Mackintosh knew that to take that many enemy combatants onto his ship was a risk, as he had no support from any other friendly vessels in the vicinity at the time, he took the decision to rescue the Germans from their perilous situation. Fortunately, by the time the rescue was complete, other British vessels had arrived on the scene. It was to one of these vessels that the Germans were transferred before being brought ashore to spend the rest of the war as prisoners. Efforts were made by the British vessels to attach a tow rope to the stricken Zeppelin so as to salvage its remains, but it broke up and sank before it was secured. It was extremely unusual for the Admiralty to deal with a situation such as this in the proactive manner in which they did, but with so many people having witnessed the events at first hand, it would have been folly to have attempted to deal with it in any other way. It was an early example of wartime propaganda.

   John Anderson, a 59-year-old Danish national, claimed he had lived and worked as a carpenter in England for some forty years. He also claimed that his five sons were all serving in the British army. In May 1916 he was fined £5 for entering the Isle of Sheppey without the permission of the registration officer. He had obtained

Head Quarters - SHEERNESS.

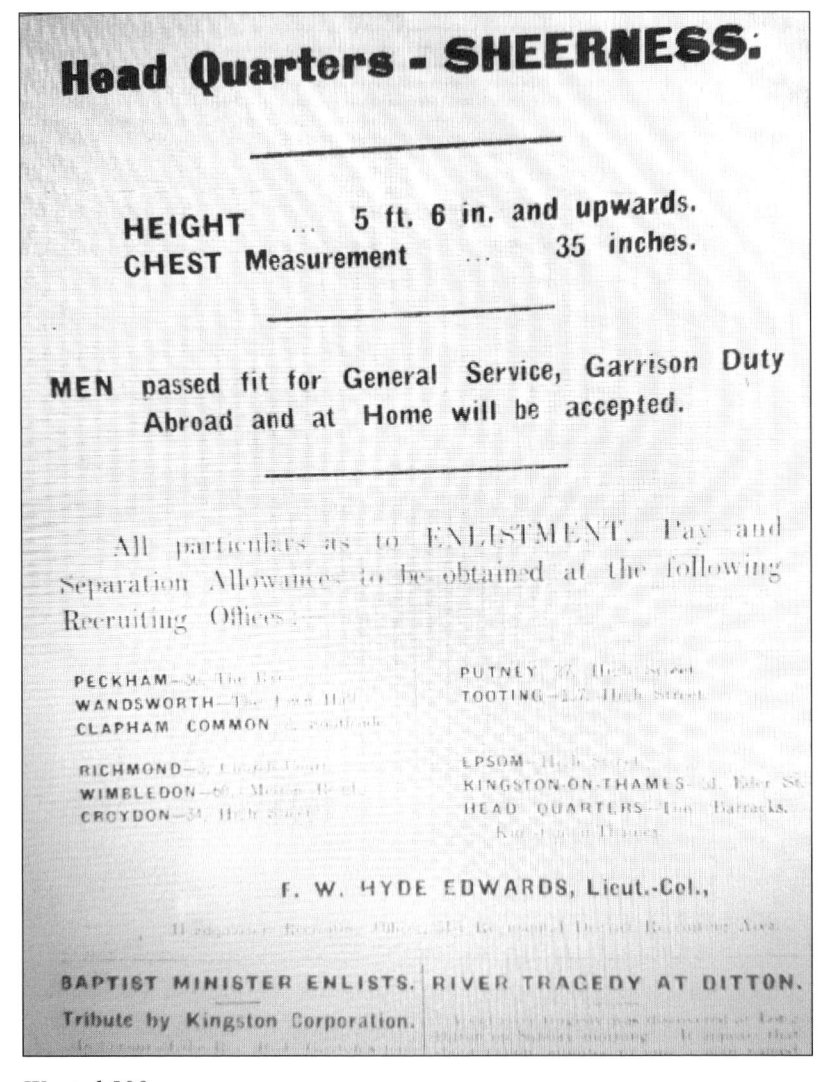

HEIGHT ... 5 ft. 6 in. and upwards.
CHEST Measurement ... 35 inches.

MEN passed fit for General Service, Garrison Duty Abroad and at Home will be accepted.

All particulars as to ENLISTMENT, Pay and Separation Allowance to be obtained at the following Recruiting Offices:

PECKHAM— PUTNEY—
WANDSWORTH— TOOTING—
CLAPHAM COMMON—

RICHMOND— EPSOM—
WIMBLEDON— KINGSTON-ON-THAMES—
CROYDON— HEAD QUARTERS—

F. W. HYDE EDWARDS, Lieut.-Col.,

BAPTIST MINISTER ENLISTS. | RIVER TRAGEDY AT DITTON.
Tribute by Kingston Corporation.

Wanted 500 men.

employment at one of the island's aviation manufacturers and had been on the Isle of Sheppey for nearly two weeks before his nationality was discovered. The island was a prohibited area to all non-British residents and had been from early in the war. The 1911 census showed a Peter John Anderson who was born in Denmark in 1852. He was a British subject, a married man who lived in Hartlepool, and by trade a timber measurer, but it only shows two sons. The restrictions on who was and who wasn't allowed to come and go from the Isle of Sheppey were accelerated in May 1916. All civilians on the island had to be registered at the local police station. They had to be in possession of their national registration card as well as their residential permit, which had to be signed by the police. If a resident was having any visitors to their home who were not also residents of the island, they had to report this to the police and provide their full details. Even more restrictive was that residents were not allowed to leave or enter the Island between 9pm and 5am.

A large advert was taken out by the government in the *Surrey Advertiser* newspaper dated 7 June 1916 asking for 500 men to enlist in the Kent Royal Garrison Artillery, whose headquarters were at Sheerness. The advertisement said that 500 men were required who were between 41 and 47 years of age. They had to be a minimum height of 5 feet 6 inches tall and have a chest measurement of at least 35 inches. Men who had been passed fit for general service or garrison duty, either at home or abroad, would be considered for acceptance. It was interesting to note that despite the fact that it was a Kent Regiment, the vacancies were also being advertised all over Surrey and London.

The same advertisement appeared in the same newspaper the following week.

In the second week of June 1916, W.J. Chave of Broadway, Sheerness, who was a special constable in the Southend-on-Sea police, was summonsed to appear before the force's chief constable to answer charges of refusing to obey an order given to him for the performance of his duties. At the time he was allocated to the Southchurch section of the town's police. On an unspecified date, Special Constable Chave left the district without informing his section's inspector, or returning his warrant card or his police-issued equipment. He was eventually discovered living back in Sheerness. He was fined one pound.

It is not known why he absented himself from his duties at Southend. The fact that he was discovered back home in Sheerness suggests that it may have been nothing more than homesickness. It isn't clear if he was made to return to his duties as a special constable in Southchurch. The 1911 census shows a Walter Chave who was 30 years of age, a tailor by profession, and a married man who lived with his wife Mary and three young children at 22 Quebec Avenue, Southend-on-Sea, which just happens to be in the Southchurch area of the town. Maybe this is the man in question.

The Dorking and Leatherhead Advertiser dated Saturday, 1 July 1916, carried the following few lines in relation to a Sheerness Tribunal:

The Sheerness Tribunal granted conditional exemption from military service to a plucky lad of 18, named Bird, a fishmonger, who is maintaining his mother, a paralysed father and three other children.

William Bird, lived with his parents William and Hannah, his brother Albert, and his two sisters Nellie and Katherine, at 10 Russell Street, Mile Town. It would appear that William junior followed in his father's footsteps as like him he was a fishmonger. The tribunal granted William a conditional exemption from having to undertake military service, and I could find no subsequent record of him hiving served during the First World War.

A financial dispute between a landlord and his tenant came before Sheerness County Court in July 1916. Mr John Murphy, a warrant officer in the Royal Navy, was successful in resisting an application for an order by his landlord for the repossession of the house which he rented from him. Mr Murphy began renting the house on 1 February 1915 for a sum of £2 10s per month, an agreement which was to remain in place until the end of that year. Then when the Increase in Rent Act became law, Mr Murphy declined to pay more than £26 per year, the amount of rent that had

1916 – THE REALISATION

been paid by a previous tenant who occupied the house when war was declared in August 1914.

The owner of the property served Mr Murphy with a notice to quit on 31 May 1916, basically because the latter had reduced the payment he had made in March 1916 on the grounds that the owner had overcharged him under the terms of the Increase in Rent Act. Judge Shortt held that the difference between £26 and £30 per year paid for the eleven months in 1915 was lost to the defendant, but held that the standard rent under the Act was the £26 paid by the previous tenant on the day preceding the outbreak of the war. The decision was an important one, making it clear that a landlord could not take advantage of a change of tenancy to increase his rent.

The *Dover Express* newspaper dated 8 September 1916 reported that notice had been given that application forms for a permit to enter or leave the Isle of Thanet, including the rural district of Sheppey, the borough of Queenborough, and the urban district of Sheerness, which was declared by an order of the Army Council that had been published on 25 August 1916 to be a Special Military Area under the Defence of the Realm Regulations, could be obtained gratis from the police. An application was to be made at the police station nearest to where the applicant lived. The island had already been declared a restricted area for foreign nationals, who were prevented from visiting, living or working in the area.

On the evening of Sunday, 22 October 1916, the following statements were issued by the Field Marshal, Commander-in-Chief, Home Forces:

A hostile aeroplane approached Sheerness at about 1.45 pm today, flying very high. Four bombs were dropped, three of which fell in the harbour. The fourth fell in the vicinity of the railway station and damaged several railway carriages. British aeroplanes went up, and the raider made off in a north-easterly direction. No casualties are reported.

Later that same evening the Secretary of the Admiralty made the following statement:

A hostile seaplane was shot down and destroyed this afternoon by one of our naval aircraft. The enemy machine fell into the sea. Judging by the time, it is probably the seaplane that visited Sheerness today.

The German version of the same attack, which was reported in an official telegram released from Berlin the next morning, was brief and slightly different:

Yesterday afternoon one of our sea-planes successfully dropped bombs on the railway station and the docks at Sheerness, at the mouth of the Thames.

I can only imagine that a British person, reading an account of the attack that they knew was written and sanctioned by an official military department, would have believed what they had read without question. Somebody in Berlin reading the official German account of the same attack in their morning newspaper would no doubt believe what they were being told as well.

The *Daily Mirror* of Thursday, 14 December 1916, reported that Second Lieutenant Frederick Hogben of the 3rd Battalion, South Staffordshire Regiment, but who was attached to the 8th Battalion, Lincolnshire Regiment, was missing in action. In one of the sad twists of the war, by the time the above information had appeared in the press, Frederick had already been dead for nearly two months. Although initially reported as being missing in action, he is officially recorded as having being killed in action on 23 October 1916 during the fighting of the Battle of the Somme. His body was never recovered and his name is duly commemorated on the Thiepval Memorial. His home was at 67 Alma Road, Sheerness, and before the war he lived there with his parents Matthew and Jessie, his two younger brothers James and Frank, his sister Jennie and her daughter Audrey. His father Matthew was an army pensioner.

Frederick's brother James Henry also served during the war, as a rifleman (6295) with the 16th Battalion, King's Royal Rifle Corps, as part of the British Expeditionary Force, first arriving in France on 16 November 1915, where he remained until returning to England on 20 April 1917. He served again in France between 12 June 1917 and 1 March 1918. After two weeks home leave between 2 and 15 March 1918 he returned to France for a third time, where he was at the time of the Armistice, finally returning home on 1 December 1918. He was demobilised on 31 March 1920 having served for more than five years with the King's Royal Rifles.

Frederick's other brother, Stephen Robert Hogben, also served during the war, as a sergeant (911016) with the Royal Field Artillery in Mesopotamia, in what is today known as Iraq. He also survived the war.

CHAPTER 5

1917
Seeing it Through

As the war continued into 1917, there was still no immediate end in sight. The battles were still coming thick and fast, with men dying in their hundreds of thousands, bringing more pain and suffering to loved ones, making parents childless, children fatherless and turning wives into widows. At least twenty-two battles took place in 1917, the bloodiest being Passchendaele and Arras, and there were numerous battles at sea.

By the end of the year at least sixteen men who had connections with Sheerness had become victims of the war.

Samuel H. Hawes was chief armourer (340701) at HMS *Actaeon* which was a name borne by both a fifty-gun hulk and a shore establishment. This was in line with the Navy Discipline Act of 1866 which required that for all shore establishments, there would be a ship afloat of the same name. Samuel was stationed at the shore establishment, which was situated at Sheerness, and he was killed during a German air raid on the town on 5 June 1917. He is buried at the Sheerness Cemetery on the Isle of Sheppey. His wife Mrs E.A. Hawes, lived at 129 Alexandra Road, Sheerness.

Harry Dryer was a stoker 1st class (SS/100290) in the Royal Navy, serving on board HMS *Faulknor* when he died on 25 September 1917. He was 33 years of age and was buried at the

Sheerness Cemetery on the Isle of Sheppey. HMS *Faulknor* was built by J. Samuel White at Cowes on the Isle of White, originally for the Chilean Navy who had ordered six large destroyers for their navy in 1912, but before the *Faulknor* could be delivered to the Chileans, the British Royal Navy stepped in and purchased it for themselves. It then spent the entire war as part of the Dover Patrol, helping to keep the English Channel safe from the vessels of the Imperial German navy. I was unable to ascertain the exact circumstances of Harry's death, and could not find out if he was killed as a result of enemy action or died as a result of an accident or illness. There were no notable incidents that the *Faulknor* was involved in on 25 September 1917 that could provide an explanation for Harry's death. His widow, Rosa Dryer, lived at 117 Alexandra Road, Sheerness. The 1911 census showed that Harry Dryer lived at 5 Blythe Court, King Street, Blue Town, Sheerness. He was the adopted son of Richard and Margaret Dryer.

Samuel Anderson was 33 years of age and a mate in the Royal Navy when he died on 16 April 1917. He is buried at the Sheerness Cemetery on the Isle of Sheppey. Samuel was a mate on HM Submarine *C16*, which had been launched on 19 March 1908. It was one of a total of thirty-eight 'C' class submarines built for the Royal Navy in the early years of the twentieth century. Samuel's is a truly remarkable story. On 16 April 1917 the *C16* was at periscope depth in waters off Harwich when it was accidentally rammed and sunk by the British Royal Navy Medea-class destroyer HMS *Melampus*. Although having sunk to the sea bed, the *C16* was still in one piece and all of her crew were still alive. In an attempt at escape the stricken vessel, Samuel was fired from one of the submarine's torpedo tubes. Whether he volunteered or was ordered to make the escape attempt is unknown. Sadly, Samuel drowned in the attempt. The submarine's commander, Lieutenant Harold Boase, made the decision to flood the boat in an attempt to allow escape through the hatch on the vessel's fore end, but sadly the fender jammed the hatch and trapped the other fifteen members of the crew, consigning them all to a watery grave. The escape attempts were discovered as a

HM Submarine C16.

result of a written note which had been placed in a corked bottle and found close to the body of the submarine's commanding officer when the vessel was later salvaged and recommissioned before being sold off for salvage on 12 August 1922. Samuel's widow, Alice Gertrude, lived at 63 Coronation Road, Sheerness.

Henry John Carroll was a local man, born at Sheerness on 2 July 1888. When the war came he enlisted in the Royal Navy and became a shipwright 1st class (345393) serving aboard the minesweeper HMS *Jason*. He was on board the vessel when it hit a mine and sunk on 3 April 1917 off the west coast of Scotland while engaged in minesweeping operations. Out of a crew of 93 officers and men on board at the time of the explosion, Henry was one of the 25 crew members who were killed. It transpired that the mine was a German one which had been laid by the submarine *U-78*. HMS *Jason* sunk in less than five minutes. Carroll's body was not recovered and his name is commemorated on the Chatham Naval Memorial. There is also a memorial to those who lost their lives that day in the Cathedral at Oban. The wording on the memorial is as follows:

> *HMS Jason was lost at 11.10am on the 3rd April 1917 off the island of Coll (latitude 56 53'N longitude 6 28'W) through striking a mine laid by the German submarine U-78 on the 11th February 1917.*

The loss was even more poignant for the people of the Isle of Sheppey as HMS *Jason*, having been converted for use as a minesweeper in 1909, was commissioned at Sheerness on 28 April 1914.

Leonard Hammett was an officer's steward 2nd Class (L/489) in the Royal Naval Reserve, serving at HMS *Wildfire*, which was a shore establishment situated at Sheerness, when he died on 17 February 1917. He is buried at Sheerness Cemetery and his widow lived at 121 High Street, Side Entrance, Mile Town.

Henry William Allison was 22 years of age when he was killed in action on 17 October 1917. He was a leading cook's mate (M/4169) on board HMS *Strongbow*. He has no known grave but his name is commemorated on the Chatham Naval Memorial. On the day in question, a convoy of nine Scandinavian coal-carrying ships was being escorted from Norway across the North Sea to a delivery port in Scotland. The escort consisted of two British destroyers in the form of HMS *Mary Rose* and HMS *Strongbow* along with the Royal Navy Trawlers HMS *Elsie* and HMS *P Fannon*. As the convoy reached Lerwick, it was attacked by two light cruisers of the German *Kaiserliche Marine*, *Brummer* and *Bremse*. HMS *Strongbow* was under the control of Lieutenant Commander Edward Brooke when, at just before 6am on 17 October 1917, lookouts spotted the advancing German vessels in the distance but initially mistook them for British cruisers. In the ensuing battle, both the *Mary Rose* and the *Strongbow* were sunk along with all nine of the Scandinavian coal-carrying vessels. Only forty-four men and four officers from the ship's complement of eighty-two officers and men survived. As well as all of the vessels from the convoy that were lost, some 250 crew were killed, which included Henry William Allison. The German vessels suffered neither damage nor loss of life, and made it safely back to their base. The attack caused a certain amount of outrage. Britain and her Allies saw it as an illegal act on neutral and civilian vessels and crew, made worse by the fact that the German vessels gave no prior warning to the Scandinavian ships which, if given, would have provided them with the opportunity to evacuate their crews before they were sunk. Henry's parents lived at 45 Maple Street, Mile Town.

Albert C. Whiting was 44 years of age and a private (28782) in the Royal Veterinary Corps when he died on 19 November 1917. He is buried at the Kirkdale Cemetery in Liverpool. His connection with Sheerness is that was where his parents John and Anna were from.

Frank Valentine Lamb, having been born in Sheerness on 14 February 1890, was 26 years of age when he died on 9 July 1917. He was an engine room artificer 3rd class (M/3806) in the Royal Navy serving aboard HMS *Vanguard*. Before he had enlisted in the navy on 27 December 1911, Frank had been a boiler maker. During his time in the navy he had also served on HMS *Diamond*, HMS *Juno* and HMS *Cressy*. Having read through Frank's entry on the Royal Navy's Register of Seaman's Services, it would appear that he survived the sinking of HMS *Cressy* by the German submarine *U-9* on 22 September 1914 before being reassigned to HMS *Vanguard*. He has no known grave and his name is commemorated on the Chatham Naval Memorial.

The *Vanguard* was at Scapa Flow in the Orkneys when the Dreadnought-class battleship was sunk by a large internal explosion. There were only two survivors: Frederick William Cox, a stoker 1st class, and John Williams, a private. Just before midnight on 9 July, one of the ship's magazines exploded. To this day, no conclusive explanation as to the cause of the explosion has been discovered, although initially, and as would be in keeping with the time, some

HMS Vanguard *at Scapa Flow.*

were suggesting that there had been foul play. Out of a crew of 900, only 187 bodies were recovered, the rest were lost to the sea, and some of those who were killed were literally blown to pieces. Frank's parents, William Bridgment and Jane Beatrice Lamb, lived at 35 Clyde Street, Sheerness.

Robert Wilcocks lived with his wife Harriet Louise at 55 High Street, Blue Town, Sheerness. When the war came he enlisted in the Royal Navy where he became a petty officer (231604). He was serving on HMS *Laurentic* when he died on 25 January 1917. His name is commemorated on the Portsmouth Naval Memorial. HMS *Laurentic* was an ocean-going passenger liner owned by the White Star Line before the war which, with the outbreak of hostilities, had been requisitioned by the Admiralty and transformed into an armed merchant cruiser. On 25 January 1917 she was on route to New York when she struck a mine off Lough Swilly near the north coast of Ireland. A total of 354 out of the 745 men on board lost their lives. Part of the ship's cargo was a large consignment of gold bullion, some forty-three tons of it, in the form of 3,211 gold ingots, which had a value of £5 million (today that amount of gold would be worth

HMS Laurentic.

£1.4 billion). It was on its way to America to pay for food, steel and munitions which the British government urgently needed to keep their war effort going. The operation to recover the gold began almost immediately, but eight months later less than one-fifth had been recovered. Once America had entered the war in April 1917, there was no longer such an urgency to recover the gold. Work to do so did not resume until two years later, and all but twenty-two bars were recovered.

The *Laurentic* was already famous for being the vessel that Inspector Dew of Scotland Yard took in 1910 to get ahead of the murderer Dr Crippen, who was fleeing to Canada on board the slower SS *Montrose*. Although the *Montrose* left ahead of the *Laurentic*, the latter arrived in Canada three days before the *Montrose*, allowing Dew to make his arrest.

Jeremiah Lynch was a chief petty officer (168671) in the Royal Navy. He was killed on 15 October 1917 at 41 years of age while serving aboard the merchant vessel MFA *Whitehead* when it was torpedoed by a German submarine in the Mediterranean. His name is commemorated on the Chatham War Memorial. His widow Annie lived at 18 Ranelagh Road, Marine Town, Sheerness.

Frank Whiddett was born in Sheerness in 1887. He had enlisted in the army in London, two months shy of his sixteenth birthday, on 4 September 1902, eventually becoming a sergeant (10221) in the 1st Battalion, Bedfordshire Regiment, although he was initially assigned to the 4th Battalion, Royal Fusiliers as private 9752. Frank married Catherine Lawless on 23 June 1908 at the Protestant Cathedral in Dublin and they had two daughters: Lilian, who was born on 19 January 1912 at Aldershot, and Veronica, who was born on 3 February 1914 in Dublin. Frank was transferred to the regiment's 6th Battalion on 10 February 1913 before transferring to the 1st Battalion on 17 April. He served in Belgium as part of the British Expeditionary Force between 14 August 1914 and 6 January 1915. On his return to the UK he was assigned to the Bedfordshire Regiment's Depot, before being discharged from the army on 6 August 1915 for no longer being physically fit enough for war service, after having served for 12 years and 337 days. Part of the report from the medical board hearing which was held on 6 August 1916 and approved his discharge from the army included the following:

> *Originated in Belgium on 30.12.14. He was taken out of the trenches on stretcher with bad cough and high temperature. Haemoptysis first occasion on 16.12.14. Had pain in upper part of chest and cough. Was invalided home. Sputum contains blood.*

The report finished with the somewhat confusing paragraph of:

> *Not result of active service, climate or ordinary military service. May be regarded as due to service since declaration of war.*

Four months before the medical board which agreed his discharge, he was already reported as being very ill. He was admitted to Downs Hospital in Sutton, Surrey, on 3 May 1916. He died of phthisis, more commonly known as pulmonary tuberculosis, or consumption, on 8 June 1917. He is buried in the churchyard of the parish church in Eaton Socon in Bedfordshire. His two younger brothers also served in the war and survived. Ernest Whiddett enlisted in the army on 3 January 1905 and became a private (6132253) in the East Surrey Regiment, while Percy John Whiddett enlisted on 30 November 1906 and became a private (11160) in the Duke of Cambridge's Own (Middlesex) Regiment. Their parents were Alfred and Ethel Whiddett.

Hugh Charles Caston was a 35-year-old company sergeant major (231) with the Kent Fortress Company, Royal Engineers, when he died of 'paralysis of the brain' on 18 June 1917. He is buried at the Woodlands Cemetery in Gillingham. On the website healthtap.com, a doctor with forty-three years' experience as a neurologist gave the following answer to the question, 'What is paralysis of the brain?'

His reply is: 'In brief, I have no idea. This is not a medical diagnosis or an accepted neurological condition.' The same website suggests the condition referred to might be cerebral palsy, as the latter of the two words comes from the latinised Greek word 'paralysis'. Hugh's widow, Mary May, lived at 161 High Street, Queenborough. Hugh was most definitely a career soldier, having been in the army for eighteen years before the outbreak of the First World War, enlisting in London on 1 August 1896 when he was just 15 years of age. His trade prior to joining the army was recorded as 'musician'. On his army service record there is a descriptive sheet which was completed on his enlistment. One of the boxes which had to be filled out was 'Distinctive Marks'. There were three: (1). Scar on forehead. (2). Eyebrows meet. (3). Brown patch on left buttock.

Caston was admitted to 'D' block at the Royal Victoria Military Hospital at Netley in Hampshire on 15 January 1915. Although the hospital catered for different conditions in wounded soldiers, 'D' block was the psychiatric ward, which dealt with a lot of men who were suffering from what had become known as shell shock (one such individual was the war poet Wilfred Owen). Caston had the following comments written about him in a medical report completed on 20 January 1915 in respect of his admission to the hospital five days earlier:

On admission he was excited, resistive, obstinate and inclined to be aggressive. Had a delusion that he was shortly going to be promoted to the rank of Major.

This was just six months into the war and shell shock had not yet been recognised as a medical condition. Point number twelve (a) on the medical report states: 'Give your opinion as to the causation of the disability.' The answer given is, 'Unknown'. Point number twelve (b) asks the question: 'If you consider it to have been caused by active service, climate, or ordinary military service, explain the specific conditions to which you attribute it.' The answer provided is, 'I do not consider that military service has taken any part in the

Netley Hospital (2).

production of the disability.' The report concludes that physically Caston is in a fair condition, that he weighs 9 stone 6 lbs, and states:

> *Patient is very restless, often gets excited if thwarted in any way. Has a delusion that he is to be promoted to Major and that he possesses great wealth. He continually asks that his motor may be sent round to take him out, also that his tailor be sent for to fit him out. States this morning that he wishes all the other patients to be supplied with Egyptian cigarettes.*

The report is completed by a lieutenant from the Royal Army Medical Corps, who states that Caston should be discharged as he is permanently unfit to undertake wartime military service. His official discharge date was on 2 February 1915.

William George Lucas was an able seaman (J/9809) in the Royal Navy, and at the time of his death on 14 February 1917 aged twenty-two, he was, according to the Commonwealth War Graves Commission website, serving on HM Trawler *Sabrina*. However, the website naval-history.net shows the *Sabrina* as a destroyer. But they are definitely referring to the same vessel as they both also mention William George Lucas, and the fact that he died as a result of accidentally drowning. His name is commemorated on the Chatham Naval Memorial, and his parents lived at 35, First Avenue, Queenborough.

Thomas Beeston was a married man who lived with his wife Elizabeth Ellen, fourteen years his junior, at 3 Stanley Avenue, Queenborough, although in April 1911 they are shown as living at 46 Nuns Road, Winchester. It would appear that they moved to wherever it was that he was stationed. They had married in 1910. By the time of his death on 19 October 1917, he was a company sergeant major (9004) with the 6th (Reserve) Battalion, King's Royal Rifle Corps, who were stationed on the Isle of Sheppey throughout the war as part of the Thames and Medway Garrison.

Arthur John Fitch was 19 years of age having been born in Queenborough in 1898. As soon as he was old enough he enlisted at Bromley in Kent and became a private (TR/10/18383) in the 29th Battalion, Training Reserve. He died of pneumonia on 12 March 1917 while in hospital at Southend and was buried at Sutton Road Cemetery at Southend-on-Sea. On the ancestry.co.uk website, under the section 'Soldiers who died in the Great War,' they show Arthur as a private (G/18383) in the 52nd (Young Soldiers) Battalion, Queen's Own (Royal West Surrey Regiment). This is incorrect on two points. Firstly, it was the 53rd Battalion that had the title of 'Young Soldiers'. I believe the reference should have been to the 52nd (Graduated) Battalion, as this had previously been the 29th Training Reserve Battalion. Secondly, both are incorrect in relation to Arthur, as both battalions were not actually formed until 27 October 1917, by which time he had already been dead for some seven months. At the time of his death the unit he was serving with

SS Nyanza.

was still known as 29th Training Reserve Battalion. The 1901 census shows Arthur, his parents William and Helen, and his younger brother Frederick, living at 30 Castle Street, Queenborough.

Richard George Barker was born in Queenborough in 1876, and during the First World War he was a steward in the Mercantile Marine on board SS *Nyanza*. He died on 9 December 1917 and his name is commemorated on the Tower Hill Memorial, which is where all of those who served in the Mercantile Marine and who have no known grave have their names commemorated.

The SS *Nyanza* was launched on Thursday, 4 October 1906, as a passenger and cargo vessel, by Caird & Company from Greenock, for the Peninsular & Oriental Steam Company. On 9 December 1917 the SS *Nyanza* was on route to Calcutta carrying a general cargo when it was torpedoed and damaged ten miles off the Lizard Peninsula in Cornwall by the German submarine *U-53* commanded by *Kapitänleutnant* Hans Rose. Richard was one of those from the *Nyanza*'s crew who was killed in the attack. During the war, Rose was responsible for sinking eighty-one Allied merchant ships, one

British warship, along with damaging a further nine allied merchant vessels.

Friday, 6 April 1917, saw the tragic death of Mr Horace Short, who was one of the early pioneers of both British flying and aircraft design. He was 44 years of age. He died in a flying accident on the Isle of Sheppey while at the controls of one of the aircraft which he had helped design. Mr Short was an engineer of outstanding ability and innovative ideas. Along with his brothers, Oswald and Eustace, he opened an aircraft factory at the Aero Club's testing ground at Leysdown in 1908, which allowed them to produce a large number of experimental aircraft. The brothers had already designed and built balloons for the Aero Club, which would later acquire the prefix of 'Royal'. In 1910 the brothers moved to nearby Eastchurch and it was there that they built the biplanes that the first four members of the Royal Navy learnt to fly in, but only after permission was granted by the Admiralty for them to do so. It was also at Eastchurch that the brothers designed and built aircraft that had more than one engine and propeller. But it was as a designer and maker of seaplanes that Horace Short was best known.

As early as 1912, seaplanes with 100 hp Gnome engines, which had been designed and built by the Short brothers, were already capable of taking off from the sea rather than land. In 1913 Horace Short came up with an invention which revolutionised the use of seaplanes, namely the big seaplane with folding wings, which enabled such aircraft to be housed in a space that was no wider than their own floats. This invention allowed for large seaplanes to be carried on relatively small ships, something which otherwise would not have been possible, and would have prevented such aircraft from being effectively used in raids on the German coastline, as well as in operations in the Eastern Mediterranean, East Africa and in Mesopotamia.

Tram cars were a part of everyday life throughout the country and had been for over a hundred years before the outbreak of the First World War. The Mumbles Railway Act was passed into law in 1804 and within three years the first tramcar system in Great Britain was up and running with the Swansea and Mumbles Railway Company. Initially the tram wasn't run on electricity but on good old fashioned horse power. Over the course of the next century these systems were developed so that horses were replaced by steam, which in turn was replaced by electricity. Some of these are still in operation today.

On the evening of Saturday, 7 July 1917, the tramcars in Sheerness stopped running for the very last time. They had been running at a loss for many years, and although they were undoubtedly an extremely helpful form of transport for a considerable number of local people, ultimately it simply wasn't quite enough to make it a viable proposition to carry on running. It was a similar story for many other tramcar systems in smaller out-of-the-way places such as the Isle of Sheppey. The tramcar had become like the lifeblood of the island's community and its removal affected many people. Without it a lot of them couldn't get out and about as they had done before and many lost their freedom and independence.

In the early hours of 6 December 1917 a German air raid which was targeted on London also brought death and destruction to the people of Sheerness, Dover and Margate. Twenty-one aircraft set out from their base in Germany, including nineteen Gotha bombers, three of which had to return to their base because of engine problems. By the time the raid was over, the German aircraft had dropped 421 bombs, the vast majority of which were incendiary. The first of the aircraft came in over the Kent coast at about two o'clock in the morning. Just over four hours later the raid was over and they were on their way back home to Germany. Only six of the aircraft made it as far as London. Three civilians and a sailor were killed in Invicta Road, Sheerness when one of the German aircraft dropped its bombs. Anne Hubbard and her son James were both killed at 141 Invicta Road; six doors away at number 129, Mrs Louisa Cox was killed; and Royal Naval Shipwright, 1st Class (347154) Horace Mouatt was killed by falling masonry.

Horace was based at HMS *Actaeon* which was a shore-based

HMS Actaeon *crew.*

establishment at Sheerness. He is buried at Sheerness Cemetery on the Isle of Sheppey. Thirty-four aircraft from the Royal Flying Corps took to the skies, but none of them managed to make contact with any of the German machines, although two of them were shot down by ground-based anti-aircraft batteries. Why no aircraft from the Royal Naval Air Service took to the skies in pursuit of the German attackers is unclear.

A meeting took place on the morning of Sunday, 23 December 1917, at Sheerness, to protest against the inefficient and inadequate warnings given to members of the public by the authorities from impending attacks by German aircraft and Zeppelins. A Mr Charles Shepherd presided, and he was supported by Mr C. Tamlyn who was the group's honorary secretary. It would be fair to say that feelings of those in attendance were running high to say the least, with most of their angst being directed against the local council. The following resolutions were passed:

(1) That we demand night warnings, bomb proof shelters for the public, and further protection.

(2) That in the event of any breadwinner being killed or disabled, there shall be a pension in case of disablement, and provisions for dependents in case of death.

(3) In the event of a worker's wife or family being ordered to leave the town by their medical attendants, owing to nervous breakdown or shell shock due to air raids, they shall receive separation allowance, the same as volunteer munition workers who have come to work in this area.

(4) That these resolutions be sent to the Prime Minister, First Lord of the Admiralty, and Secretary of State for War.

In addition, it was agreed that representations would be made to the local council for them to provide a motor ambulance for the town. The general feeling was that the local council had not done much in the way of even thinking about, let alone having taken any measures, to cope with air raids.

Resolution number three was somewhat of a corker, which dare I suggest, hadn't been properly thought through. Now, I fully accept that being the recipient of a bombing raid by enemy aircraft isn't going to be top of the list of things to have on a 'bucket list' of must-do experiences, but I find it somewhat implausible that being subject to one enemy air raid, that is going to last for a matter of minutes, is going to be sufficiently traumatic to result in a civilian being suddenly struck down with shell shock. Let us take stock for a moment and think of the common soldier on the Western Front, stuck in a trench, with nowhere to go while enemy artillery shells are raining down on him and his buddies. He looks to his left and a friend is killed, blown to pieces by an exploding shell. He looks to his right, and a colleague slumps backwards as his head is blown clean off his shoulders, and still the shells rain down on their position and continue to do so, for hour after hour, day after day, in the cold and rain, made worse by sleep deprivation and lack of food. A man crouched in a corner, in an effort to make himself as small as he possibly can, while praying that the next explosion isn't going to have his name on it. Now that would be a justifiable and believable reason to claim you were suffering from shell shock.

When reading these pages, it should be remembered that they do not contain every single incident which occurred on the Isle of Sheppey during the war, but what is recorded here is more intended to provide you, the reader, with a flavour of the events of those bygone days. Everyday life, or rather what passed for it, went on across the Isle of Sheppey, just like it did in thousands of villages, towns and cities up and down the country. People had to go to work, very often women, while looking after their children and running a home. It wasn't easy, and for many of them they had the added worry of knowing that they had a loved one fighting somewhere in the war.

CHAPTER 6

1918
The Final Blow

❖

1918 was to be the final year of the war, and by now everybody was tired and fed up and just wanted the bloody and barbaric fighting to be over with as soon as possible. But before the final curtain could come down to end the madness of the previous four years, even more battles would have to be fought and won.

The Battle of the Lys, also known as the Fourth Battle of Ypres, took place between 7 and 29 April 1918. It was a German offensive with the ultimate objective of capturing the Belgian city of Ypres, forcing British forces back to the coast and, more importantly for Germany, out of the war. That was the plan, but thankfully for Britain and her Allies, the Germans came up short. It took soldiers from eight countries to defeat them. Besides the Commonwealth countries of Britain, Australia, Newfoundland and Australia, troops from Portugal, Belgium, France and the United States of America were also involved in the fighting to defeat the Germans.

Although referred to as the Battle of the Lys, the twenty-two days of fighting actually consisted of eight smaller battles, which began at Estaires on 9 April and finished at Scherpenberg on 29 April.

During the period 7 to 29 April 1918, at least seven men who had connections with Sheerness were killed.

Edward Howting was 19 years of age and a private (27806) in

Battle of the Lys, gassed soldiers.

the 7th Battalion, King's Shropshire Light Infantry, when he was killed in action on 22 April 1918. He had enlisted at Eastchurch, where he was born, and had previously served as a private (10/25988) with the regiment's Territorial Reserve Battalion. He has no known grave, but his name is commemorated on the Loos Memorial in the Pas-de-Calais. Before the war Edward had lived with his parents, Edward and Caroline, at White Post Cottage, Eastchurch, Sheerness. There were five other children of the marriage. Sons James, Henry, William and Albert, along with daughter Charlotte, who was the youngest. William (mentioned later in the book), who was the middle of the five brothers, had been killed in action on 10 October 1917 while serving on the Western Front in France.

James Alfred Sellen was 32 years of age and a private (41488) in the 1st/7th Battalion, Middlesex Regiment, when he was killed in action at Arras on 11 April 1918. He is buried at the Dainville Communal Cemetery in the Pas-de-Calais. His parents, Jesse and

Battle of Arras.

Martha, lived at 49 East Lane, Blue Town, in Sheerness. James had two younger brothers, Thomas and Harry, and a sister, Ethel. Harry, who would have only just reached his 18th birthday in 1918, was a sapper, WR/125187, with the Railway Section of the Royal Engineers. Harry had possibly not even finished his initial training by the time of the Armistice.

The Battle of Arras was between British, Canadian, Australian, New Zealand and Newfoundland forces, against the forces of the German Empire. It lasted from 9 April until 16 May 1917 and saw the British and Commonwealth Forces attack German defensive positions around the French city of Arras. It was seen as a British victory, but the thirty-eight days of fighting resulted in 158,000 Allied casualties, an average of 4,158 for each day of the fighting.

It is estimated that German losses were between 120,000 and 130,000 men.

John Edward King was 22 years of age and a private (75519) in the 22nd (Tyneside Scottish) Battalion, Northumberland Fusiliers, when he was killed in action on 10 April 1918, having first arrived in France on 20 August 1914. He had begun the war serving in the Army Service Corps as a driver (CHT/572). Transferred to the Duke of Wellington's (West Riding) Regiment, he became Private 33508, before eventually ending up with the Northumberland Fusiliers. He has no known grave but his name is commemorated on the Ploegsteert Memorial in the Hainaut region of Belgium. His parents lived at 26 Bell Alley, Mile Town, Sheerness.

Richard Wood was 37 years of age and a private (G/52302) in the 2nd Battalion, Royal Fusiliers, when he was killed in action on 13 April 1918. His body was never recovered and his name is commemorated on the Ploegsteert Memorial. His parents, Mr and Mrs William Matthew Wood, lived at 20 St Georges Avenue, Mile Town. Richard had four brothers, Robert, Frederick, Edward, and Walter. Robert was 37 years of age and a civilian shipwright employed at HM Dockyard in Sheerness when he was killed on 27 May 1915 while working on board HMS *Princess Irene* when she exploded and sunk.

Arthur Sharland was 28 years of age and a private (55678) in the 6th Battalion, Welsh Regiment, when he was killed in action on 24 April 1918. He had previously served as a private (32283) in the Norfolk Regiment. Fouquières-lès-Béthune is a village which can be found about half a mile outside the town of Bethune. Private Sharland is buried in the Fouquières Churchyard Extension. His parents, John and Frances, had lived at 16 Harris Road, Mile Town, which had been the family home for many years. Even after John's death in 1909 at the age of 57, Frances kept the house on so as to bring up her seven children, five sons and two daughters. Albert was the middle of the five sons. Bertie and Albert were too young to have served in the war, and I could find nothing about either John or William having served in any branch of the military during the war.

Thomas Rouse Underdown was 29 years of age and a private (248103) in the 2nd Battalion, London Regiment (Royal Fusiliers), when he was killed in action on 24 April 1918. He had initially enlisted as a private (268108) in the Hertfordshire Regiment before transferring to the Middlesex Regiment and eventually ending up in the London Regiment. He is buried at the Hangard Wood British Cemetery in the Somme region. His parents, Thomas William and Esther, lived at 3 Railway Cottages in Queenborough, and his widow, Florence Amy, lived at Scocles Farm, Minster, Sheerness. Thomas had two younger brothers, Edward and Bertie. Edward Richard Underdown served with the Royal Engineers as a sergeant (256828) (WR/269308).

Edward Charles Turner was a 27-year-old lance corporal (45960) in 'C' Company 19th Battalion, Lancashire Fusiliers, when he was killed in action on 25 April 1918. He is buried at the Lancashire Cottage Cemetery in Hainaut. Before the war he had been a labourer working in the fields of many of the nearby farms to where he lived. His parents, John Richard and Kathleen, lived at 22 Castle Street, Queenborough. Edward was the eldest of their three sons, then came Ernest who was five years younger, and last but not least was the youngest by three years, Jack. John had previously served in the British Army, and at the time of the 1901 census he was shown as being in the Portsmouth Military hospital, and as a corporal in the Army Reserve. Kathleen was not the boys biological mother. She and Richard had married in 1903.

The Battle of the Marne was an Allied counter-offensive of the Marne region, which came under the control of the French commander, General Ferdinand Foch, and took place between 20 July and 2 August 1918.

During this time there were two men connected to the Sheerness area who became victims of the war.

Ernest Edward Davis was only 19 years of age. He was a private (G/21877) in the 6th Battalion, The Buffs (East Kent Regiment), when he died of his wounds on 27 July 1918. He is buried at the Delville Wood Cemetery, at Longueval in the Somme region. Just after the First World War, his parents, William and Johanna, lived at 97 Coronation Road, Sheerness. They had previously lived at 3 Alexandra Road in the town. Ernest's father William was a Kent man who worked as a gas fitter's foreman, a well-paid job which provided a good standard of living for him and his family. Besides Ernest there were two other sons, Albert, who was the eldest, and William, who was the youngest, and too young to have taken any part in the war. I could find no record of Albert having served in the military during the war, which isn't to say that he didn't. He had obviously decided to follow in his father's footsteps when it came to work, as, at 15 years of age, he was working as a gas fitter's mate.

Robert Lewis Bushell also lost his life during this time. He was killed in action on 2 August 1918, but his death was not connected to the Battle of the Marne. Robert was 31 years of age and an

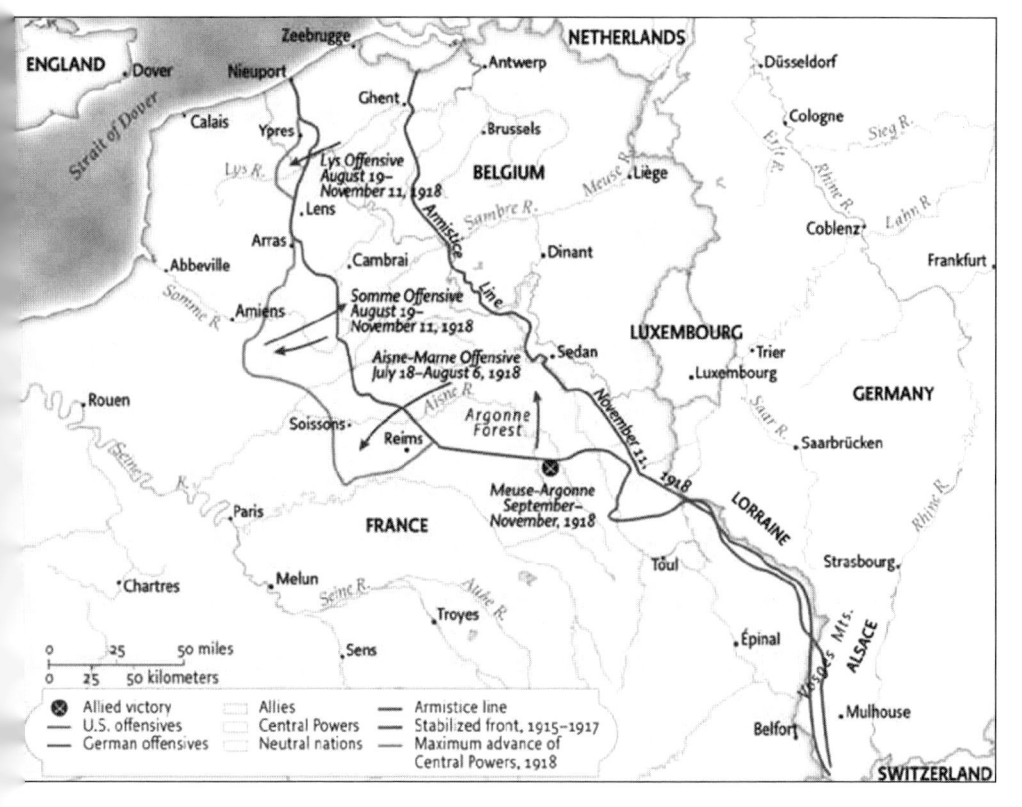

Map 1: Western Front as of 11 November 1918.

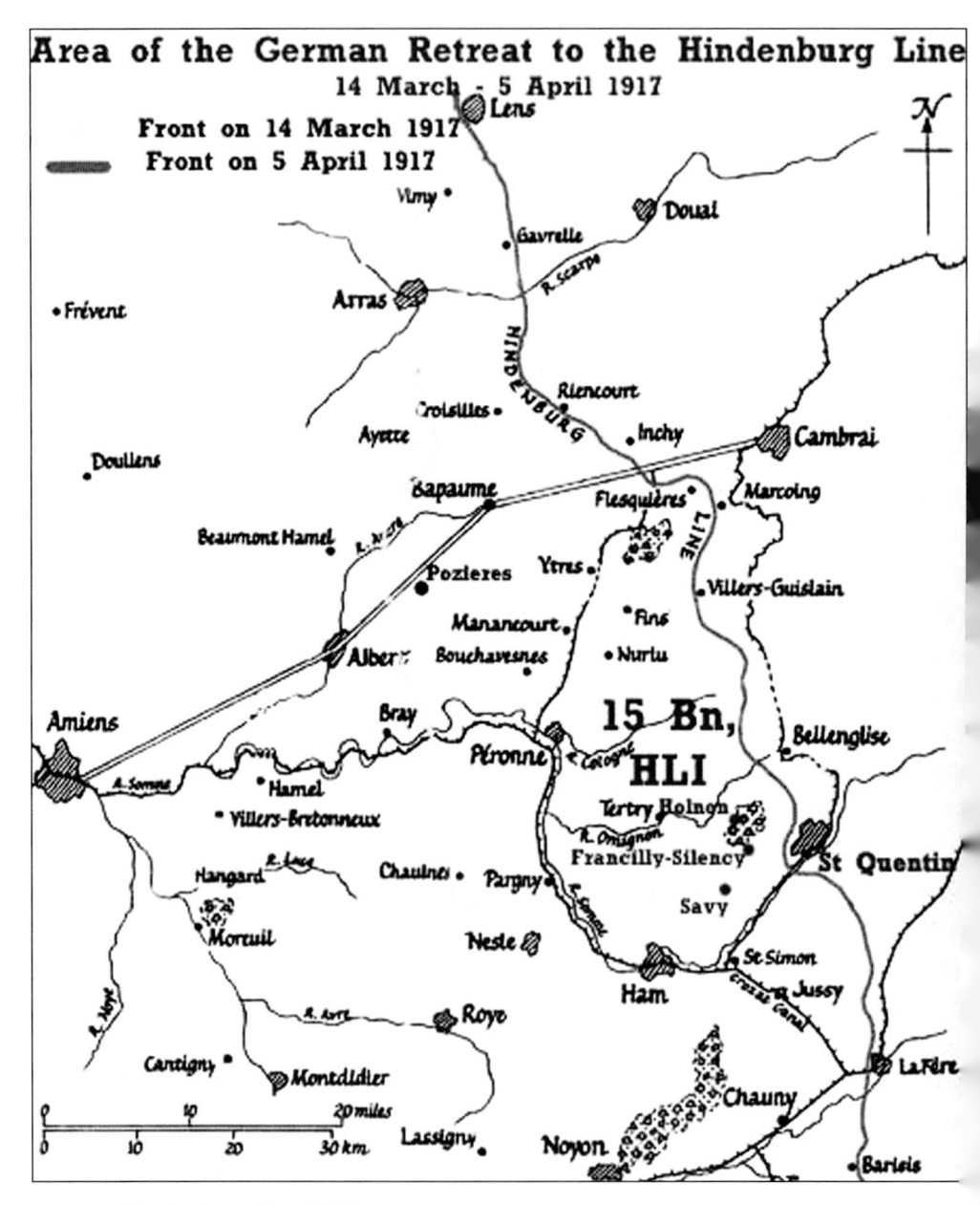

Hindenburg Line 1917.

officer's steward 1st class on board HMS *Aeril* when she struck a German mine and sunk, taking forty-nine members of her crew, including Robert, to a watery grave.

The main event of 1918 as far as Britain and her Allies were concerned, and what ultimately determined the final outcome of the First World War, was the 'Hundred Days Offensive'. In essence this was a series of offensive battles which pushed German forces out of France and back behind the Hindenburg Line, which was a German defensive position built during 1916-17.

The offensive began with the Second Battle of the Somme which took place between 8 August and 3 September 1918 and was a British and Allied response to the German Spring Offensive, while at the same time being part of the Allied Hundred Days Offensive. It included troops from Britain, Australia, Canada and the United States. The Second Battle of the Somme was made up of the Battle of Amiens, the Battle of Albert, the Second Battle of Bapaume, the Second Battle of Arras, the Battle of Mont St Quentin, and the Battle of Peronne. The offensive consisted of numerous quick-fire battles as the Allies continued to push German forces further and further backwards into a full-scale retreat, which didn't stop until the signing of the Armistice on 11 November 1918.

During this time a total of nineteen men connected in one way or another with the Isle of Sheppey were killed during those final four months of the war. For a relatively small community such as theirs, this was a staggering loss of life, which affected so many other people, immediate family, relatives, friends and colleagues.

George Thomas Yates was 28 years of age and a sergeant (46005) in the 26th Siege Battery, Royal Garrison Artillery, when he died of his wounds on 15 September 1918, having first arrived in France on 4 August 1915. He was buried at Sheerness Cemetery. George came from a big family, even by the standards of the time. He was the eldest of ten children born to George and Elizabeth Yates, who, according to the 1911 census, lived together at Sayes Court Cottages, in Harty on the Isle of Sheppey. George had six brothers and three sisters. Of his brothers, five of them, Alfred, William, Percy, Frederick and Charlie were all old enough to have served during the war.

William was just shy of his twenty-first birthday when he enlisted at Chatham on 16 January 1915 and became a driver (041513) in the Army Service Corps. Prior to this he had worked as a farm labourer. After having completed his initial training, he was sent out to France from Southampton on 28 January 1916, arriving at Le Havre the next day, where he remained until 5 September 1917 when he was given a twelve-day period of leave. The following year he received a sixteen-day furlough, on 30 September. He returned to the UK to relax and see friends and relatives, only to then have to return to his unit, the 234th Heavy Transport Company in France. It would be another five months before he saw home again, returning to his family on 25 March 1919, before being finally demobbed at the No.2 disposal unit at Crystal Palace on 22 April 1919 and placed on the Army Reserve. By now the family was living at Rayham Farm, Eastchurch.

Percy, who was only 19 years of age, not only enlisted into the Army Service Corps as a driver on the very same day as his brother William did at Chatham, but they also had consecutive service numbers, with Percy's being 041514. They even travelled out to France on the same day. They were allocated to the same unit, given the same leave periods, and returned to the UK at the war's end on the same day. They were even demobbed on the same day at Crystal Palace. They really were in every sense, brothers in arms. The only difference on his service record was a disciplinary matter dated 8 April 1918, when he received a punishment of being confined to camp for five days for committing the offence of 'wilful waste of Government property, in pouring a quantity of motor oil on a pie'. That really is a true story! Having taken a look at the inventory of kit that Percy was issued with on enlisting, wedged between 'Hose tops, pairs... and Knifes' was a 'Housewife', which he apparently returned to the stores when he was demobbed.

Frederick also served, as a gunner (153693) in the Royal Horse

Artillery. That's all the information I could find on Frederick's military service, although because of his age he couldn't have legally enlisted until 1916. He also survived the war. I could find no record of either Alfred or Charlie having undertaken military service during the war.

Henry William Miles, 22 years of age, Private (3080638), 5th Battalion, Canadian Mounted Rifles. He was killed in action on 6 November 1918, dying instantly after being shot by German machine gun fire while taking part in the attack and capture of Crespin. He is buried at the Onnaing Communal Cemetery, Nord, France. He was born on the Isle of Sheppey, but when he was only 12 years old his parents, Walter and Mary, decided to make a fresh start and, along with Henry and the rest of their young family, emigrated to Canada, arriving in Quebec on 2 July 1909 on board the SS *Virginian*. The 1911 Census of Canada showed a much larger Miles family living at 1302 Notre Dame Street, East Montreal: Walter John (Father), Mary (Mother), and children Walter John (19), William (14), Henry (4), Wilfred (2), Lilly (20), Mary (18), Rosa (11) and Grace (8). Henry is shown as only being 4 years of age, which I can only assume is a typo, as by 1911 he would have actually been 14 years of age.

Edwin Charles Holmes was 22 years of age and a private (G/15298) in the 7th Battalion, Queen's Own (Royal West Kent Regiment) when he was killed in action on 19 September 1918. He is buried at the Unicorn Cemetery at Vendhuile which is situated in the Aisne region of France. His parents, Mr and Mrs E.J. Holmes, lived at 159 High Street, Queenborough, although in the 1911 census the family was shown as living at 89 High Street, Queenborough. Before he enlisted, he was an 'assisting fat refiner' for a chemical manufacturer. He had two brothers, Cuthbert and Alfred, along with two sisters, Cissie and Annie.

Cuthbert enlisted in the Royal Navy on 7 February 1917 and was demobbed on 5 March 1919. The ship he was serving on at the time was HMS *Indomitable*, a vessel which had an illustrious wartime career, having seen active service at both the Battle of Dogger Bank and the Battle of Jutland.

HMS Indomitable.

George Thomas Hopkins was 21 years of age and a private (T/270291) in the 10th (Royal East Kent and West Kent Yeomanry) Battalion, The Buffs (East Kent Regiment), when he was killed in action on 21 September 1918. He has no known grave and his name is commemorated on the Vis-en-Artois Memorial. By the end of the war his parents, George Thomas and Mary, and George's three sisters, Clara, Hilda and Gladys, lived at Melita House, High Street, Queenborough, and prior to this the family home had been at 8 The Street, Iwade, Sittingbourne, Kent, where George worked as a labourer on a local farm.

A.E. Wood was 27 years of age and initially a private (29890) in the Middlesex Regiment, before he was transferred to 437th Agricultural Company, Labour Company. He died of his wounds on 4 November 1918, just a week before the signing of the

Armistice. His widow, Lilian Mabel, lived at 2 School Lane, Blue Town.

Charles Horswell was only 18 years of age and a private (G/31801) in the 1st Battalion, Queen's Own (Royal West Kent) Regiment when he was killed in action on 27 September 1918. He has no known grave and his name is commemorated on Vis-en-Artois Memorial. He was born on 19 December 1899 at Dumbarton Castle, while his sister, Louisa, was born in Sheerness on 4 May 1905. After the war his parents, Edward and Georgina, lived at 47 Granville Road, Mile Town. They had married on 23 July 1891 in Edinburgh, even though after their wedding they were living at 6 Chapel Street, Bluetown, Sheerness.

Despite being 51 years of age, Edward enlisted on 8 April 1915 and became a gunner (282029) in the Royal Garrison Artillery, having previously served with the same regiment in his younger years. He was transferred to the Army Reserve on 6 November 1916 and discharged in full on 14 December 1918, having been deemed surplus to military requirements.

A. Jordan lived with his father at 14a North Star Passage, Sheerness. He wasn't involved in the Hundred Days Offensive, but he was still a local man who died during the course of 1918, so I felt it was only right and proper to mention him here, even if only briefly. He was a driver (54219) with the 69th Battery, 19th Brigade, Royal Field Artillery when he died on 10 October 1918 while serving in Greece. He is buried at the Mikra British Cemetery in Kalamaria in Greece.

Charles Edward Butler was 31 years of age, a married man who was a private (34198) in the 1st Battalion, Devonshire Regiment, when he was killed in action on 20 October 1918. He is buried in the Bethencourt Communal Cemetery which is situated in the Nord region of France. His widow Martha lived at 2 Jefferson Road, Sheerness, although the 1911 census had showed the couple as living in Gloucestershire, which is the part of the country where they both came from, and how they came to be living on Isle of Sheppey is not clear.

Thomas Robert Batchelor was a married man who lived at 26 Granville Road, Sheerness, with his wife Nellie Winifred. His parents, Thomas and Louisa, also lived in the town. With the coming of the war, Thomas enlisted in the army and worked his way up to the rank of sergeant (31062) in the 59th Siege Battery in the Royal Garrison Artillery. At 28 years of age he died of disease on 31 October 1918 and was buried at the Mont Huon Military Cemetery in the coastal town of Le Treport, which during the war became a notable medical and hospital centre for Allied servicemen.

William Reuben Bass was born in Sheerness in 1893. With the outbreak of war, he enlisted and eventually became a corporal (35245) in 'L' Anti-Aircraft Battery, which was part of the Royal Garrison Artillery. Having first arrived in France on 1 December 1914, he was killed in action on 2 September 1918, at which time he was 25 years of age. He is buried at the Bellacourt Military Cemetery in the district of Rivière in the Pas-de-Calais. The 1911 census showed William as living at 28 Broad Street, Sheerness, with the Holmes family and his father, Reuben, who by then was 64 years of age and an army pensioner. By trade William was a milkman. Ten years earlier he had been living with his three elder sisters, Caroline, Mary and Florence, at their auntie's home at 5 South Street, Sheerness.

Charles Jempson was 30 years of age and a private (G/9358) in the 1st Battalion, The Buffs (East Kent Regiment), when he was killed in action on 8 October 1918. He is buried in the British Cemetery which can be found just south of the village of Montbrehain. His parents, Charles and Emily, lived at 3 Clarence Row, Sheerness. He was the youngest of four children, with two brothers, Sidney and Frederick, and his sister Flora. I could find no record of Sidney having served during the First World War, but I did find a Frederick C. Jempson who served as a private (L/7543) with The Buffs, (East Kent Regiment) before transferring to the Labour Corps, where he was an acting corporal (197999). I could not establish with any degree of certainty if this was the same Frederick Jempson I was looking for.

Frederick George Thomas lived with his parents, Frederick and Ada, at 4 Granville Road, Sheerness, which made him a close neighbour of Thomas Robert Batchelor, who lived in the same street at number 26. Prior to this the family had lived at 3 Short Street, Mile Town. He was the eldest of three children, with sister Gladys and brother Horace making up the family. Frederick was a private (38688) in the 1st Battalion, Norfolk Regiment, when he was killed in action on 27 September 1918. He was just 18 years of age. He has no known grave and is commemorated on the Vis-en-Artois Memorial, which is situated in the Pas-de-Calais.

George Robert Howard was also a private (38686) in the 1st Battalion, Norfolk Regiment, his service number suggesting that he enlisted on the same day as Frederick George Thomas. Sadly, the coincidences didn't stop there, as he was killed on the exact same day as Frederick. His home was at 24 Granville Road, Sheerness, so they lived in the same street as each other. This also made George the next door neighbour of Thomas Robert Batchelor who lived at number 26. At the time of his death, George was 24 years of age. He was buried at the New British Cemetery which is situated on the outskirts of the village of Gouzeaucourt, which is in the Nord, France.

I was undecided whether or not to include the next man, as his connection to the Isle of Sheppey was tenuous to say the least. Here is his story. You decide. It would appear that he was from Herne Hill and that his only connection with the island was his wife moving there after the war: Reginald Thomas Mellish was 32 years of age and a gunner/signaller 1st class (205091) at the Signal Training Depot (Fareham) in the Royal Garrison Artillery. He died of influenza while serving in England. At the time of his death he was a patient in 'Hut 2' at the Alexandra Military hospital in Cosham, Portsmouth, having been admitted there on 23 October 1918. His condition was so bad by the time he was admitted, that he died later the same day.

He was a married man, having wed Christeen Matilda Blanch Carter on 30 October 1915 at St Pauls Parish Church in Thornton

Heath. Five weeks after his wedding, on 9 December 1915, he enlisted in the army, and the next day he was placed on the Army Reserve. He was not mobilised until 18 March 1918. After her husband had died, Christeen moved to 'Horeview', Sexburga Drive, Minster-on-Sea, Isle of Sheppey.

Harry George Levy lived with his parents Harry and Maria at 44 St Vincent Terrace, Sheerness. Prior to this they had lived at 44 Rose Street, Mile Town. He was the eldest of three children, with a younger brother Frederick, who was two years his junior, and sister Louisa who was five years younger than him. Harry enlisted in the army during the war and became a gunner (96054) with the 24th Division's Ammunition Column, Royal Field Artillery. He was killed in action on 17 October 1918 at the age of 23 and was buried at the Delsaux Farm Cemetery, near the village of Beugny in the Pas-de-Calais.

Archibald Herbert Ashenden was 26 years of age and a sergeant (G/23693) in the 7th Battalion, Royal Sussex Regiment, when he was killed in action on 8 August 1918. He is buried at the Beacon Cemetery at Sailly Laurette in the Somme. His parents, Herbert and Susan, lived at Sheerness, and his widow Eveline lived at 23 Cross Lane East in Gravesend. The 1911 census shows Archibald as a single man living with his parents at Clifton House, Halfway, Minster, Isle of Sheppey, and his profession as assistant school master. He was the eldest of three children, being two years older than his brother Ronald Francis Brenchley and five years older than his sister Gladys Ursula Pricilla Jean. Ronald also served during the war as a private (39164) with the 1st Battalion, Leicestershire Regiment. He enlisted on 25 July 1916 and was discharged due to sickness, rather than being demobbed, on 13 February 1919. Despite the war being over he was still issued with a Silver War Badge, No. B.185592.

William Alfred Bolton was 30 years of age and a gunner (821396) in 'A' Battery, 282nd Brigade, Royal Field Artillery, when he was killed in action on 29 September 1918. He is buried in the Windmill British Cemetery at Monchy-le-Preux in the Pas-de-

Calais. His widow, Maud Lilian, lived at 78 Alma Road, Sheerness. The 1911 census showed William living at his mother Emily Bolton's address of Luton Road, Harpenden in Hertfordshire, where he was a collar ironer. Also living with them was one Maud Lilian Bozier, the future Mrs Bolton.

Thomas A. Stone was born in Australia. By the time of his death on 14 October 1918, his widow Emma was living at 16 Coronation Road in Sheerness. He was 25 years of age and a corporal (334056) in the Royal Garrison Artillery when he died on 14 October 1918.

Henry and Ellen Miles, the parents of Harry William Miles, lived at Sheerness. As the war began, Harry was living with his wife Jessie in Poplar, East London, and he enlisted becoming a Private (6617) (533361) in the 15th (Prince of Wales's Own Civil Service Rifles) Battalion, London Regiment; later he transferred to the Regiment's 12th (The Rangers) Battalion. He died of wounds he received during fighting at Cambrai, while serving in France on 29 October 1918. He is buried in the Cambrin Military Cemetery in the Pas-de-Calais.

The Battle of Cambrai lasted from 20 November until 7 December 1917, and was an attempt by British, Commonwealth and American forces to capture the French town of Cambrai, which was an important supply point for Germany's Hindenburg Line. Both sides suffered casualties in the region of 45,000 men; the British lost 179 tanks.

A large meeting took place in Sheerness on Sunday, 27 January 1918, consisting of representatives of the engineering and shipbuilding professions along with those from the National Union of Railwaymen. The war had just entered its fifth year and despite all the losses, not only was there no immediate end in sight but the army was demanding more and more men to carry on fighting the war. At the end of 1917 the War Office estimated that the army had a shortfall of 70,000 to 80,000 men, and that by the end of October 1918 that figure would rise to nearly 250,000 men. Haig and his staff believed that this figure might even be twice that amount at around 460,000.

Battle of Cambrai.

What the meeting at Sheerness highlighted was the growing unrest amongst the masses on the issue of more and more men being required by the army to go and fight in the war. There was a loathing in some quarters of the army generals, whose poor tactics and apparent lack of understanding of how to fight a modern war was seen as the real problem, especially as, rather than being prepared to overhaul their approach, they seemed intent on just sending more and more young men to their deaths.

The army generals for their part were also unhappy as they were now faced with a government which no longer seemed prepared to support their needs, while still expecting them to deliver a final and glorious victory which would then no doubt be claimed by the politicians as their own achievement. Nowhere was this made clearer than with the findings of a government committee which had been set up to look at the nation's overstretched manpower situation. Not one person from the army had been invited to sit on that committee. The findings of the committee were set out in the form of a list of the top four areas of need of national manpower requirements as they saw it:

(1) The fighting needs of the Royal Navy and the Royal Air Force.
(2) Shipbuilding.
(3) Tank and aeroplane production.
(4) Food production and timber felling.

Nowhere was there any mention of the army's needs.

The representatives from the different civilian unions present at the meeting demanded immediate peace negotiations be commenced on the basis of no annexations or indemnities and self-determination of nationalities, and pledged itself, failing this, to take action, with other organised workers, against the Man Power Bill. Similar meetings took place across the country, with some making much stronger political statements and demands.

On Friday, 22 February 1918, the driver of a motor vehicle from Sheerness was ordered by the Faversham County Court to pay damages for a collision he was involved in with a horse and trap. The sum of money involved was £7 15s 9d. His Honour, Judge Shortt, heard how Mr Ernest Hills, a grocer, was suing Mr W.H. Sadler, an assistant civil engineer at Sheerness Dockyard, for damage to his trap and some eggs. The claim related to an incident which had taken place on 5 May 1917, when the car that Mr Sadler was driving crashed into the trap, damaging its off-side wheel. The force of the collision was such that it knocked Mr Hills' daughter out of the trap along with some eggs which then smashed on the ground. Mr Sadler stopped to assist Mr Hills' daughter, but in part only to point out to her that the accident was her fault. Mr Hills' daughter took the index number of Mr Sadler's vehicle and subsequently wrote to him requesting that he pay for the damage, a letter which Mr Sadler decided not to reply to because, as he stated to the court, he thought it was no more than an attempt by Mr Hills to try to extort money from him. It was Mr Sadler's refusal to answer Mr Hills' letter that had resulted in the matter ending up in court. Having listened to both sides make their case, Judge Shortt found in favour of the plaintiff, Mr Hills, ordering Mr Sadler to pay him the full amount that had been claimed.

To give these matters some perspective, and by doing so not suggesting in any way that the incident didn't deserve to be treated as seriously as it was, on the day of the accident, 5 May 1917, a total of 1,133 men of the British and Commonwealth forces died of wounds, illness or disease, or were killed in action.

Thursday, 23 May 1918, saw a very important person visiting Sheerness: none other than King George V, when he made a planned visit to Chatham and Sheerness dockyards. The king met with members of his armed forces, members of the Scouts and the Girl Guides, WAACs, WRENs and other war-related workers. He was also keen to meet and chat with ordinary members of the public and find out about their lives and work. It was evident throughout his visit, especially when meeting his loyal subjects, that they were very pleased to see him, as he was them. He made it known that he had thoroughly enjoyed the experience.

At Chatham he was offered lunch by some of the port's naval officers, but, although grateful for the offer, he politely turned it down, instead taking lunch on his train, something which he had intended to do all along, where he ate a strictly rationed light meal.

On route to another destination after lunch, and while his train was waiting in a siding, he was introduced to the train's driver, William Waters, who had been an engine driver for thirty-seven years, during which time he had driven members of the Royal family, including the king, on many occasions. Four of Mr Waters' sons had enlisted, two had been killed, one was missing and a fourth was serving in France. The king offered Mr Waters his heartfelt thanks and deepest sympathy for his loss and the price that his family had paid in serving him and a grateful nation.

The *Western Times* newspaper, dated Wednesday, 26 June 1918, carried a report about the Mayor of Exeter awarding the Imperial

Service Medal to Mr William Wickenden of 95 Oakhampton Road, Exeter, for 42 years and 10 months' service. The medal was inscribed on the back with the words, 'For faithful service'. The 1911 census shows that the man was in fact Joseph William Wickenden, who was born in Sheerness in 1857. He had lived in Sheerness all of his working life before moving to Exeter on the occasion of his retirement in 1918. His last address in Sheerness was 11 St Georges Road, and his working life had been spent as a tool smith in the ship-fitting shop at Sheerness Dockyard. He and his wife Amelia had married in 1880 and she had borne him ten children, one of whom had died during infancy. I could not find any information about any of Joseph's three sons having served during the First World War.

On the evening of Wednesday, 24 July 1918, Private William Allen, of the Royal Engineers, and who was attached to the light railway worker's unit, arrived home on leave from France for the first time in sixteen months, having served on the Western Front for nearly all of that time. He was the stepson of Mr Walter Williams, a game keeper, of 'Shacklands', Shoreham, Sevenoaks, and prior to enlisting in the army he had been a clerk at the Sheerness railway station. During his time in France he had experienced the trauma which went with having been gassed, but thankfully for him it wasn't a fatal experience; he just had to rest up for a few days before returning to his unit.

Monday, 16 September 1918, saw the unfortunate death of Commander Charles Walter Campbell Strickland of the Royal Navy, who was serving at HMS *Wildfire*, a shore base at Sheerness Dockyard where he had been stationed since 22 June 1918. While returning a seaman's salute at a railway crossing, he stopped on the railway line and was hit by a passing train which he had failed to see. He died in hospital at Sheerness from multiple injuries. A newspaper report of the time records his death as having taken place on Monday, 16 September 1918, while the Commonwealth War Graves Commission websites shows it as having been on Saturday, 14 September 1918. He was 46 years of age, a married man, and survived by his wife Constance and their two daughters Constance and Katrina. He is buried at Charlton Cemetery in Greenwich.

Edward Charles Clarke was a private with the Royal West Kent Regiment, stationed at Leysdown on the Isle of Sheppey. On Friday, 27 September 1918, he was placed before the Sevenoaks Petty Sessions, the chairman of which was Mr P.F. Battiscombe. Also sitting on the bench with him were Sir William Plender, Sir Douglas Fox, Reverend C.G. Ashworth, and Mr F. Swanzy. Police Sergeant C. Saunders informed the court that at about 0900 hours that morning he had attended at 10 Redman's Place, Sevenoaks, where he had seen Private Clarke and asked him if he was absent without leave from his regiment, to which he replied that he was. He further admitted that he should have returned to his barracks at Leysdown nine days earlier, on 18 September. Sergeant Saunders then detained him and escorted him back to Sevenoaks Police Station in readiness for his court appearance. The bench ordered that he be remanded in custody so that a military escort could attend and return him back to his barracks at Leysdown. His punishment for this breach of military regulations was a forfeiture of pay for nine days. Sadly, he didn't learn his lesson, as just nineteen days later he was once again absent without leave, this time for eleven days. His pay was once again docked for the period of time that he had been absent.

Private Clarke's story was an interesting one. He was born in Wrotham in 1894 and enlisted in the army on 16 January 1911 at Sevenoaks, when he had only just turned 17 years of age. He became part of 'G' Company, 3/4th Battalion, Royal West Kent Regiment, which was a territorial unit and which had previously been the 1st Volunteer Battalion, Royal West Kent Regiment. On the outbreak of war, he was undergoing his annual period of military training with his Territorial unit. These exercises usually took place over a two-week period, but because of the start of the war, the 1914 manoeuvres only lasted for nine days, from 27 July to 4 August, when they returned to their barracks at Leysdown. His Territorial service number was 1086, but no sooner had Edward and his colleagues returned from their annual training camp, than he was suddenly discharged for being medically unfit, his last day of service being the 18 September 1914, after having served for 3 years 246 days. There are no details or any specific information showing what was wrong with him that resulted in him being medically discharged. British Army service records for the First World War are not always clear, or even in a chronological order, which sometime makes them hard to follow. Although Edward's record clearly shows him having being medically discharged from his Territorial unit on the date mentioned above, he then somehow managed to re-enlist in the 2/4th Battalion, Royal West Kent Regiment, Territorial Unit on 12 October 1914, twenty-four days later, as Private 24594. On 30 December 1916 he was posted to the Regiment's 7th Battalion. On 4 September 1918 he was posted to the 5th Battalion, followed by the 6th Battalion on 20 November 1918, and finally to the Depot Battalion on 14 December 1918. He was finally discharged on 20 May 1919, which meant that he had served for a further 4 years 142 days. At the bottom of his 'Statement of Service' page, was typed the following: 'DISCHARGED-surplus to Military requirements (having suffered impairment since entry into the service.)' He had served in France as part of the British Expeditionary Force between 30 December 1916 and 29 October 1917, and then again from 20 November 1918 until 13 December 1918. Captain R. Anstruther, who was the adjutant of the 7th Battalion, Royal West Kent Regiment, wrote the following report about Edward, dated 14 August 1917. He sent it to the Officer in Charge, Regular Infantry Section No.5, GHQ, 3rd Echelon:

In reply to your memo attached hereto; I have made enquiries and the following is a statement as near as can possibly be ascertained of No. 24594, Private Clark(e)'s previous service.
    Enlisted sometime in July 1909 at Sevenoaks.
    Old Regimental No. was 1061.
    Posted to 4th Battalion, Royal West Kent Regiment, 'G' Company.

> *He was due for discharge in July 1913, but re-enlisted for a further period of one year.*
>
> *A few days before he became due for discharge in July 1914, he was admitted to hospital and remained there until after war broke out.*
>
> *When he was discharged from hospital he re-joined his Battalion (4th, Royal West Kent Regiment). He did not make any enquiries about his discharge papers thinking that under the circumstances he would have to continue to serve.*
>
> *The 4th Royal West Kent Regiment was ordered to India and he was passed unfit, he was then transferred to the 2/4th Battalion and remained with them for a few weeks until they were ordered abroad, when he was once again passed as being unfit and transferred to the 3/4th Battalion and from there to the 4/4th Battalion. He joined this Battalion with a draft from the 4/4th Battalion in April of this year.*
>
> *I trust the above information will assist you in clearing up this matter.*

Far from clearing anything up, it appears to have made matters worse. He did in fact enlist at Sevenoaks but on 16 January 1911, not 'sometime in July 1909'. Private Clarke's name has an 'e' in it, and his service number was 1086 and not 1061. There is no mention in the report concerning Edward having being discharged from the army on 18 September 1914 for being medically unfit. There is no explanation as to why he was admitted to hospital in July 1914, and why he was subsequently deemed to be medically unfit to undertake front line duties, yet fit enough to remain in the army. What makes the comment about him being admitted to hospital at the end of July 1914, where he remained until after the outbreak of the war, somewhat confusing, is that his army service record also shows that between 26 July and 4 August 1914 he was in fact undergoing his annual Territorial Army training summer camp at Longmoor.

CHAPTER 7

Those Who Didn't Come Home

◆⋮⋮◆

The Commonwealth War Graves Commission website shows the details of twenty-nine men from the Isle of Sheppey who were killed or died as a result of their involvement in the First World War. This isn't the complete list for the island by any means as the same website also includes separate lists of men for Sheerness, Leysdown, Eastchurch, and Minster.

I thought it would be useful to look at the twenty-nine men from the Isle of Sheppey in a bit more detail.

William Howting was 24 years of age and a private (40944) in the 2nd Battalion, Essex Regiment, when he was killed in action on 10 October 1917 during fighting on the Western Front. He has no known grave and his name is commemorated on the Tyne Cot Memorial, West-Vlaanderen. Before the war William was a farm labourer and initially he had enlisted as a private (24513) in the Northamptonshire Regiment, before later transferring to the Essex Regiment. Williams parents, Edward and Carrie, lived at White Post Cottages, Eastchurch. There were four other brothers, James, Henry, Albert and Edward. Sister Charlotte was the youngest of the six children.

Edward (mentioned earlier) was also killed during the war, on 22 April 1918 in France, aged 20. A double loss for the Howtings to have to endure, made worse because neither of their sons' bodies were ever recovered to give them a proper burial. Knowing that their sons were dead must have been bad enough, but to know that they were just lying in a field undiscovered must have made the grieving much harder to deal with.

Albert Victor Murdock was a private (L/9394) in the 2nd Battalion, The Buffs (East Kent Regiment), having enlisted on 31 October 1910 at Canterbury when he had just turned 18 years of age. He was based in the UK until 18 February 1911, when he was sent out to Dublin, where he remained until 10 November 1913, when he was posted to India, where he remained until 15 November 1914, when he returned to the UK, before being sent out to France on 17 January 1915. He was initially reported as being missing in action on 25 May 1915, before being confirmed as having been killed in action three days later. He has no known grave and his name is commemorated on the Ypres (Menin Gate) Memorial in West-Vlaanderen. His mother, Elizabeth Charlotte, who at the time of Albert's death lived at Station Road, Eastchurch, wrote a letter to the Infantry Records Office in Hounslow, dated 25 June 1915. In it she said the following:

> *Sir,*
> *I received news on 14th June from one of the 1st Gordon's that my son Albert, 9394, was found outside their trench shot through the back and they retrieved him the best they could. Any further particulars, I would be glad to hear.*
> *Yours respectfully*
> *Elizabeth Murdock*

Sadly, it would appear that Albert had been dead for more than two weeks before his mother was informed of his death, and then not through official channels but in a letter from an officer of another regiment. Sometime later, Elizabeth moved to 4 Coastguards Cottages, Leysdown. Two of Albert's brothers also served during the war. Henry was in the Royal Navy, stationed at Chatham, and Hubert, like Albert, was in the 2nd Battalion, The Buffs (East Kent Regiment) and was stationed at Bombay in India.

James Shrubsole (mentioned above) was 29 years of age and a private (G/8144) in the 6th Battalion, The Buffs, (East Kent Regiment), when he was killed in action on 3 July 1916, the third day of the Battle of the Somme.

Alexander John Crampin was 27 years of age and a gunner (177789) in the 76th Siege Battery, Royal Garrison Artillery, when he died of his wounds on 13 December 1917. He is buried at the Lijssenthoek Military Cemetery, West-Vlaanderen. His parents, George and Alice, lived at 4 Windmill Terrace, Minster, although in the 1911 census George is shown as being a hotel owner, specifically the Highlanders Tavern, High Street, Minster.

Henry William Miles (mentioned above) was 22 years of age and a private (3080638) in the 5th Canadian Mounted Rifles Battalion when he was killed in action on 6 November 1918, just five days before the signing of the Armistice. Before the war and becoming a soldier, Henry had been a blacksmith, which certainly meant that he was more than comfortable working with horses. He was born on the Isle of Sheppey but when he was 12 years old his family emigrated to Canada. He is buried at the Onnaing Communal Cemetery.

John Thomas Warren was 40 years of age and a skipper in the Royal Naval Reserve. He was serving on HMS *Arctic Whale* when he died on 23 November 1919, more than likely from illness. He is buried at the Scartho Road Cemetery in Grimsby. His parents John and Sarah lived at Minster on the Isle of Sheppey.

William Henry Castle was only 19 years of age and a private (G/5462) in the 2nd Battalion, The Queens (Royal West Surrey Regiment) when he was killed in action on 25 September 1915. He has no known grave, but his name is commemorated on the Loos Memorial in the Pas-de-Calais. Before the war he held the somewhat relaxing and peaceful occupation of under gardener. He was the eldest of six children, three brothers, Charles, Albert and George, and two sisters, Emma and Hilda. They lived with their parents at Holmwood, Seathorpe Avenue, Minster.

Walter Charles Sims was 21 years of age and a lance corporal in the Machine Gun Corps (Infantry) when he died on 28 March 1917.

He is buried in the Skopje British Cemetery in the Republic of Macedonia. His widow lived at Sparrow Cottage, Brambledown, Isle of Sheppey, although prior to this the family had lived at 6 Willsons Cottages, High Street, Hoo, near Rochester.

James Thomas Munn was 30 years of age and a petty officer stoker serving on HMS *Godetia*, an Arabis-class sloop launched in 1916, when he died on 22 April 1920. He is buried in the Weston Mill Cemetery in Plymouth. He had previously served in the Dardanelles and the Persian Gulf. His parents, Tom and Elizabeth, lived at New Hook Cottage, Minster.

A search on the same website on the name of Leysdown comes up with the names of four men from the town who died during the war, three of which, Murdock, Shrubsole, and Whish, are mentioned above. The other one is interesting for a different reason.

Alfred Ernest Stickings was 43 years of age and a sergeant (4863) in the 20th Divisional Company of the Army Cyclist Corps when he died on 24 June 1918. He is buried in All Saints Churchyard, Eastchurch on the Isle of Sheppey. Alfred had previously served in the army during the Second Boer War as a king's sergeant, but by the time the First World War came around he had retired. He enlisted on 14 September 1914, but six months later, on 10 April 1915, he was discharged from the army under Paragraph 392 (111cc) King's Regulations. Under this section, men with between three and six month's service, and who in the opinion of the deputy director of medical services, an assistant director of medical services, or a medical inspector of troops, feels that they are unlikely to become efficient soldiers, may be discharged.

The same website records the details of a further seven men from Eastchurch who were also killed during the war. I have already written earlier about William and Edward Howting, George T. Yates, Alfred John William Newman, Thomas Rogers, and George Ernest James Norman. The seventh is Sergeant H. Walker. He died after the end of the war, on 20 February 1919, and is mentioned later.

The Commonwealth War Graves Commission website records a total of eleven people from Blue Town who were killed or died during the war. I have previously mentioned Private Boother, Private Deadman, Private A.E. Wood, Robert Wilcocks, James Brown and George Arthur Packer.

Special mention is warranted for the only female from the Isle of Sheppey who died while in military service. She was 19-year-old Ada Emeline Martin who died on 30 April 1919 while serving as a member (25645) in the Women's Royal Air Force. She is buried at Sheerness Cemetery on the island. Her parents, Alfred and Eleanor Martin, lived at 17 Charles Street, Blue Town. Besides Ada, they had three other children, Eleanor, Alfred and Ethel.

George Phillips was 22 years of age and a private (3403) (201037) in the 1st/4th Battalion, Essex Regiment, when he was killed in action on 26 March 1917. He is buried at the Gaza War Cemetery. His parents William and Emma lived at 4 Bentham Square, Blue Town.

The First Battle of Gaza took place on 26 March 1917. It involved the British-led Egyptian Expeditionary Force trying unsuccessfully to capture the Ottoman-held town of Gaza. The one day of fighting resulted in the deaths of 523 British soldiers, with a further 512 who were missing and a staggering 2,932 who were wounded. The Ottoman forces and her allies had 316 of their men killed, 641 of them recorded as being missing, and 750 wounded.

John Edwin Henry Jeans was 19 years of age and a private (30963) in the 2nd Battalion, Devonshire Regiment, when he died on 31 May 1918. He has no known grave and his name is commemorated on the Soissons Memorial, which is in the Aisne region.

The war diaries for 2nd Battalion, Devonshire Regiment, show that on Friday, 31 May 1918 they were in trenches at Rouchy, but at 0030 hours that day they were ordered to move to the rear. On doing so, the rest of the day was spent reorganising and resting. There is no mention of any officers or men having been wounded or killed on that day. On Thursday, 30 May 1918, the battalion had been forced to retreat from the ridge where they were, owing to the fact that the Germans were attempting to get around their right flank. The tactical withdrawal was successful, ending with the battalion

Battle of Gaza.

Soissons Memorial.

reaching the Ardre Valley and repelling all German counter-attacks while incurring 'very few casualties'. It is more than feasible that Private Jeans was one of those wounded on 30 May and that he died of his wounds the following day. His father, William John Jeans, lived at 72 High Street, Blue Town.

Frederick Pack was 34 years of age and a private (228221) in the 1st Battalion (London Regiment), Royal Fusiliers, when he died of his wounds on 8 June 1917. He was a single man who was a farm labourer before enlisting in the army. He is buried at Lijssenthoek Military Cemetery. His parents, Thomas and Martha, lived at 27 Charles Street, Blue Town. His younger brother Alfred also served during the war, as a private in two different regiments. He initially enlisted into the East Surrey Regiment, where his service number was 34129. From there he was transferred to the Royal Fusiliers as Private 228222.

Harry Ledger was 23 years of age and a private (24510) in the 2nd Battalion, Northamptonshire Regiment, when he was killed in action on 4 March 1917. He is buried at the Fins New British Cemetery at Sorel-le-Grand. Both his parents, Harry and Harriet, and his widow, Nellie, lived in Sheerness, the latter at Sunshine Cottage, Edward Street, Blue Town. The 1911 census shows Harry living with his aunt and uncle at 250 High Street, Blue Town.

The same search engine on the Commonwealth War Graves Commission website records 181 men who were either from Sheerness or who had a connection in some way with the town, and who died as a result of their involvement in the First World War. As there are so many of them I am simply going to list their names in alphabetical order:

Ackhurst, Arthur Albert
Allison, Henry William
Allison, Robert
Argent, John William
Ashenden, Archibald Herbert
Austen, Frederick

Ayre, John
Back, Harold Herbert
Bailey, Ernest E
Bailey, Frederick A
Baker, Edward James
Barker, Frederick Addaman

Barling, Henry William
Barling, Nathaniel Thomas
Barton, Arthur
Bass, William Rueben
Batchelor, Thomas Robert
Batt, Albert
Beal, John Thomas
Beardoe, Herbert William
Beer, Frank John
Beer, Richard Martin
Blee, John Francis
Borthwick, George
Bridges, Sidney Augustus
Bromley, John Richard
Brown, Frederick William
Brown, James
Brown, R
Brunger, William George
Burrows, Robert Andrew N
Butler, Charles Edward
Cackett, Horace James
Cakebread, Horace Jasper
Callaghan, Stephen
Carpenter, Ernest George
Carroll, Henry John
Caryer, Ernest Charles
Cheeseman, Harold Montague
Chittick, William
Chrisfield, Frederick James
Clackett, Frederick Sherlock
Clanford, Albert Thomas
Collingbourn, John Albert
Conroy, H E
Cox, Frederick George
Davie, George
Davies, S H
Davis, Ernest Edward
Dawe, Cyril Arthur William
Deal, Alfred Joseph
Dennison, William Webster
Dering, Frederick Charles
Dryer, H
Dunn, William Edward
Edwards, Frederick William
English, George Herbert
Evans, Alfred Owen
Evans, George Mafeking
Fardell, Henry Nelson
Fisher, Arthur Thomas
Fisher, Charles Richard
Fittall, W T
Foreman, Henry George
Foulkes, William Henry
Francis, F
Franklin, George
French, Albert
French, Thomas Edward
Gamblin, William
George, Ernest Foster
Gilbert, Frederick James Charles
Gilbert, J T
Girvan, Daniel
Goldfinch, Arthur
Gordon, Robert
Goulding, John Dryden
Grant, John George
Gregory, Frederick
Halls, C H
Hammett, L

Hamnett, Arthur Septimus
Hancock, Harold Claude
Harris, William Alfred
Harrison, William Hugh
Hassell, Sydney Headon
Hide, David John
Hodges, Henry Thomas
Hogben, William
Hooker, Bertram Harold
Hopkins, Charles Henry
Horswell, Charles
Horwood, Frederick John
Howard, George Robert
Howard, John George
Howell, Reginald Arthur
Hunt, George William
Hunter, Thomas
Irons, Richard Victor
James, Albert
Jempson, Charles
Jenner, Reuben William Edward James
Johnston, Robert
Jordan, A
Kimber, Edward John
King, John Edward
Laine, Arthur
Lamb, Frank Valentine
Lawrence, Henry Charles
Levy, H G
Lissenden, A S
Lynch, Jeremiah
Mann, William Horace
Marden, Charles
Martin, Frank
Mason, A G
Matthews, Albert Edward
May, Albert John
McMahon, J P
Meakin, George Ernest
Mellish, Reginald Thomas
Mercer, H
Moore, F
Murby, Alonzo
Noakes, Robert
Nokes, Frederick Charles
Nokes, Henry
Pack, William
Parnham, R J
Paston, George Thomas
Peacock, William James
Pettitt, William
Pink, William
Price, Stanley Ernest Walter
Proom, Thomas
Purdy, Thomas Henry
Quicke, Herbert Cowper
Rawlinson, Frederick Ernest V
Reed, Richard Martin
Reed, W J H
Richardson, George
Roberts, Albert Rossell
Roberts, Clifford Edward
Rogers, John Robert
Rowswell, Bertie
Samuel, Vernon James
Saunders, Frederick Charles
Scarfe, John William
Sellen, James Alfred
Sewell, Henry John

Sharland, A
Sheer, Frank
Sheers, William Frederick
Slade, George Henry
Smith, William
Snelling, Horace
Steele, Ernest
Stephens, Joseph Henry
Stirling, Robert
Stone, T A
Stride, John Stanford
Sullivan, Edward Austin
Susans, William Thomas
Tenwick, George Frederick
Thirkettle, Victor Arnold N
Thomas, Frederick George
Thompson, Edward
Thompstone, John Henry
Thurgood, John Edward
Trowell, Edward Thomas
Vousden, George William
Wade, William Swift
Walker, H
Waters, Thomas Robert
Whiting, A C
Wilcocks, Robert
Wilson, Alexander Mackintosh
Wiseman, Archibald
Wood, Matthew Thomas
Wood, Richard
Wood, Robert

I do not suggest that the above list is either a complete or a comprehensively correct record. It is purely what came up when inserting the name 'Sheerness' in to the 'Additional Information' box in the search engine on the Commonwealth War Grave Commission's website. Their list actually has 224 names on it, but I have already covered some of these men whose names came to light when searching on other locations in the Isle of Sheppey.

The next list has been arrived at by using the same website, but this time placing the town of Minster into the search engine 'Additional Information' box. It came up with thirteen names, while other names that could have been claimed by Minster are recorded as being natives of, or as having connections with, Sheerness:

Austen, Frederick
Bailey, Frederick J
Brightman, Wesley
Castle, William Henry
Crampin, Alexander John

Gilbert, Frederick James Charles
Irons, Ernest
May, Albert John
Mellish, Reginald Thomas
Munn, James Thomas
Taylor, Frederick Charles
Underdown, Thomas Rouse
Warren, J T

As there were no criteria laid down by officialdom as to how a man warranted being named on a particular war memorial, there was never going to be any guarantee that some would be missed off altogether. Others were placed on more than one memorial, while some had their names spelt incorrectly and some men either served under a pseudonym for a number of different reasons.

The Sheerness War Memorial was unveiled by Sir Hugh Evan-Thomas, who was the commander-in-chief at the Nore, on Saturday, 29 April 1922, during a ceremony which began at 3pm. The prayers and service were shared between the Reverend E.F. Tozer from the Alma Road Congregational Church, Reverend C.J. Chamberlain of the YMCA and Baptist Church, the Reverend R.J. Lubbock who was the vicar of St Paul's Church in Sheerness, and the chaplain of the church in HM Dockyard at Sheerness. One of the other dignitaries present on the day was Councillor W.J. Thwaites JP who was the chairman of the Sheerness War Memorial Committee. The cost of the memorial was funded out of voluntary subscriptions and donations received from members of the local community. Below are the men and women from the Isle of Sheppey who fell during the years of the First World War and who are named on the Sheerness War Memorial. I have not included those who were lost when the HMS *Princess Irene* exploded and sunk, as their names have been recorded elsewhere in this book:

Navy

Allison, H W
Allison, R

Anderson, S
Atkins, L

Sheerness War Memorial.

Ayre, J
Barker, F A
Barling, H W
Beer, F J
Bentley, W J
Bickford, F W
Blore, B W
Bloxham, J A W
Borthwick, G
Boys, W H
Bridges, G T
Brinkley, T
Brunger, W G
Bushell, R L

Carroll, H J
Coltart, W
Cole, S F L
Cooley, W J
Cox, F G
Denison, W W
Dering, F C
Dryer, H
Dunn, W F
Edwards, C
Ellis, F
Evans, A O
Evans, C A
Evans, C M

Faulkes, W H
Faulkner, C H
Franklin, C E
Furber, C J
Futcher, A S
George, R F
Glenister, H
Hammett, L
Harfoot, F
Hide, D J
Hodges, H
Hooker, B H
Innes, D C
Jackson, E R
Johnston, R
Justice, M
Kitchener, W T
Lamb, F V
Lovell, A A
Lynch, J
Mason, J
McDonald, D
Meakin, C E
Mitson, A
Moore, H J
Moore, W W
Moriarty, T

Noakes, R
Oldbury, F
Onslow, A G (DSC)
Oakwell, T
Paston, G T
Poney, H
Pratt, C H
Purdy, T H
Richardson, C
Roberts, A
Roberts, C
Scarfe, J W
Sinclair, R J
Sparks, E
Sutton, L
Thurgood, J E
Tidmarsh, A H
Till, W
Tredgett, J H
Waters, T R
Webb, F C
White, E V
Whitehouse, J
Williams, F A
Wilson, A
Wood, G
Wood, A

Army

Ayling, W
Baillie, A P
Bastow (MM), E J
Batchelor, T R
Batt, A G

Barnard, A H
Barnard, H J
Bass, W R
Beer, W S
Body, F W

Body, J C
Boother, J
Brown, A V P
Blunt, D H
Campbell, H F
Campbell, J C
Carpenter, E C
Chaplin, W E
Chrisfield, F J
Claringbold
Cole, J B
Coleman, S F
Conroy, H F
Cork, W
Copland, R W
Cotteridge (DCM), A J
Crampin, A J
Davie, (DCM, MiD), G
Davis, E E
Day, R
Deadman, E P H T
Deadman, E D
Debbage, B J
Dixon, E
Donovan, B
Durbin, W W
Dyason, J N
Etoe, C
Farren, P
Fisk, F
Fittal, W T
Foreman, H C
Francis, F
Freeman, H
French, T E
Friday, J E

Gilbert, F J
Gaines, W
Gilbert, W P
Goldfinch, A J
Goldsmith, W T
Gooding, C A
Gordon, R A
Griesel, H G
Griffiths, D W
Hay, C E
Hammond, W F
Hancock, H
Harmes, A
Harmes, T
Harding, A E
Hayward, E
Hayward, T W
Herbert, A
Hirst, D W
Hopkins, C H
Hogben, F
Hogben, W J A
Horswell, C F
Howard, C R
Howard, J G S
Humphrey, J
James, A
Jempson, C
Johnston, T C
Jordan, A E
Jordan, F D
Jullien, W P
King, H
Kingston, W P
Ledger, H
Lissenden, A S

Litchfield, A
Macdonald, A
Major, C A
Martin, F
Matthews, A E B
McMahon, F P
Miles, E
Milton, A H R
Molloy, C
Moore (DCM), F
Moore, L J
Moore, W
Muckleston, G T
Murdock, A V
Newman, H J
Northcott, C H
O'Grady, J A S
O'Grady, J O S
O'Grady, M J
Ormsby, R H
Oxford, P
Pack, F
Pack, S
Parker, C A
Parnham, R J
Pearce, R J
Peed, J T E
Percival, A C
Phillips, A E
Powis, A
Prescott, W
Price, S W J
Reed, R M
Redpath, H E
Regnall, T
Richards, R F

Ride, H J
Rowswell, B
Saunders, F G
Searle, G
Sellen, J A
Sharland, A
Shepherd, E G
Sherriff, F L
Shoesmith, J
Smalley, A J
Smith, A E
Smith, C A
Smith, R W
Sole, E
Sosbe, J
South, T J
Stone, J
Stonham, C T
Sugg, J H
Taylor, F C
Tenwick, C T
Thirkettle, G H
Thirkettle, J
Thirkettle, V A N
Thomas, F C
Thompstone, J H
Turk, H J C
Twigg, F H
Vousden, C W
Wallace, C R
Ward, H L C
Wells, C R
Westacott, E H
Westbrook, H
Whiting, A
Williams, A W

Williams, F J H
Winter, L A
Wishart, W
Wood, A
Wood, C D

Wood, H
Woods, T J
Young, C S
Young, H

Air Force

McCudden, W T M
McCudden (MC), J A
McCudden (VC, DSO, MC), J B M

Killed in Enemy Aircraft Raids
Navy

Davies, J D
Gandy, M
Hawes, S H

Hibben, C
Mouatt, H H
Winmill, A

Army

Amos, Rif
Corby, Pte
Galley, Rif

Smith, Pte
Tapper, Rif

Citizens

Cox, L J
Frier, G
Hubbard, J F

Hubbard, M A
Lucas, H H
Perry, E P

Excluding the civilians who were killed in the explosion of the *Princess Irene*, there are the names of 267 men and women inscribed on the war memorial at Sheerness, although I am not totally clear as to why the McCudden brothers, brave and heroic men that they were, have been included as I cannot find any connection they have with the town.

CHAPTER 8

The Aftermath

A post war Great Britain was an interesting place to be for all concerned. The world had changed and things were never going to be quite the same again.

People had just come through four and a half years of bloody war, which in one way or another affected every family throughout the nation. Everybody had made some kind of sacrifice to help in the victory against Germany and her allies. The working classes didn't want to go back to how it had been for them before the war; they wanted to see change, they wanted a better life, and the sacrifices they had made to mean something real and tangible.

For some the war didn't end immediately the Armistice was signed. It was never going to be quite as simple as 'the war's over boys, down tools and go home.' Many men in the army were not demobilised straight away as they were needed in the different theatres of war to ensure a smooth transition into a productive and peaceful postwar Europe. For these men demobilisation was going to be on average six months further down the road, before they would get home to be with their families.

The harbinger of death didn't cease his activities just because the war ended. Between 12 November and 31 December 1918 a total of 19,295 men died, through illness or wounds they had received during the war. Eight of these men came from the Isle of Sheppey.

John George Howard was 23 years of age and a private (39527) in the 8th (Service) Battalion, Queen's Own (Royal West Kent Regiment) when he died of pneumonia two weeks after the signing of the Armistice, on 25 November 1918. He is buried at the Étaples Military Cemetery in the Pas-de-Calais. Étaples was the site of a massive wartime British base, used both as a camp for mainly British soldiers, as well as being a major medical centre which included a convalescent depot, four Red Cross hospitals, one stationary hospital and eleven general hospitals. It could cater for as many as 22,000 sick or wounded troops at a time. At the end of the war, John's parents, William and Alice, lived at 20 Clyde Street, Marine Town, Sheerness, but at the time of the 1911 census they were living at 18 St Vincent Terrace, Halfway Houses, near Sheerness, with their nine children. Alice had given birth to another four children who had died during their infancy. Including John there were six sons and four daughters.

Alfred, the eldest of the children, and William's son from a previous marriage, had completed his military service four years before the war had begun. He had enlisted in the navy on 17 January 1898 and ended up as a stoker 1st class (354614), with his last day of service being 22 January 1910. Although by then he was only 32 years of age, he was not required to rejoin the navy at the outbreak of the war.

Horace served as a private (G/21190) with the 10th (Kent County) Battalion, Queen's Own (Royal West Kent Regiment) and survived the war.

Charles Sidney Young was 22 years of age and a private (270468) in the 10th (Royal East and West Kent Yeomanry) Battalion, The Buffs (East Kent Regiment), when he died of influenza on 15 November 1918. He is buried at the Ascq Communal Cemetery which is situated in the Nord region of France. His parents, Thomas and Annie, lived at 9 Harris Road, Sheerness, and besides Charles they had two other sons, Frederick, the eldest and Edwin, the youngest. Edwin served as a stoker 1st class (K.4426) in the Royal Navy during the war and survived, living to the age of 63.

William Thomas Fittall was 20 years of age and a private (98559) in the 1st Battalion, Middlesex Regiment (Duke of Cambridge's Own). One of forty-six battalions which the Middlesex Regiment raised during the course of the war, it was also known by the nickname of the Die Hards. William died of his wounds on 30 November 1918 and is buried at the Étaples Military Cemetery. His parents, Edward and Elizabeth, lived at 168 Invicta Road, Sheerness. William's brother Edward was six years older than he was and an apprentice at HM Sheerness Dockyard, but I could find no record of him having served during the war. Maybe he was not conscripted because he was working at the dockyard.

Harold Claude Hancock was 29 years of age and a gunner (358251) in 'M' Battery, 155th Anti-Aircraft Section, Royal Garrison Artillery, when he died on 20 November 1918. He is buried at St Sever Cemetery Extension in the town of Rouen. His parents Richard and Louisa lived at 11 Russell Street, Mile Town, with their other son William George and their daughter Lilian Louise.

Victor Arnold Norman Thirkettle was 25 years of age and a driver (38241) in the 282nd Army Field Artillery, Signal Subsection, Royal Engineers. He first arrived in France on 19 November 1915 and died 26 November 1918. He is buried at the Denain Communal Cemetery. Denain is a town in the Nord region of France where, from 1 November 1918 to 12 March 1919, the 33rd Casualty Clearing Station was posted. Prior to this it had been a major medical centre for the Germans. Victor's widow, Edith May, lived at 5 Grandville Road, Sheerness.

Robert Brown was only 16 years old and a signal boy (J/89978) in the Royal Navy serving on HMS *Ganges* when he died on 29 November 1918. He was born in Sunderland and is buried at the Sheerness Cemetery on the Isle of Sheppey. At the end of the war, his mother Isabel Harris, formerly Brown, was living at 58 Winstanley Road, Sheerness.

Alonzo Murby was 29 years of age and a corporal (39651) in the 17th Battalion, Hampshire Regiment, when he died on 27 November 1918. He is buried at the Sheerness Cemetery. Although

Alonzo was born in Nottingham in 1888, his widow Alice lived at 31A Rose Street, Sheerness. In the 1911 census he is shown as already being in the army, as a private (7753) in the 4th Battalion, King's Royal Rifle Corps. He first arrived in France on 13 August 1914, making it all the way through the war before dying two weeks after the signing of the Armistice.

George Davie was 37 years of age and a company sergeant major (300006), in the 1st/7th Battalion, Essex Regiment. He was the holder of the Distinguished Conduct Medal, as well as having been mentioned in despatches. He died of dysentery on 25 November 1918. He is buried in the Beirut War Cemetery in the Lebanon. He was born in Sheerness and at the end of the war his parents, Frederick and Caroline, still lived in the town, while his widow, Alice Mary, lived at 32 Blackstone Road, Dalston, London.

James Richard Sellen was 30 years of age and a sergeant (17428) on one of the Royal Air Force's training squadrons when he died at the Ipswich Military Hospital in Suffolk on 17 December 1918. He is buried in the churchyard of the Holy Trinity Parish Church in Queenborough. There is also a record on the German deaths and burials 1582-1958 database which shows a 30-year-old James Richard Sellen, who was buried in Baden, Germany on 23 December 1918, just six days after James died. The 1911 census shows James as a bricklayer and a boarder with the Macbain family, who lived at 4 Railway Terrace, Queenborough. His widow, Maud Clair Victoria Sellen, lived at 20 Alsager Avenue, Queenborough.

Instead of reducing, the number of Britons who died as a result of the war more than doubled in 1919, to a total of 38,340. Of these, nine men and one woman had connections with the Isle of Sheppey, Thomas Hunter was a 19-year-old private (206083) in the 1st Battalion, London Regiment (Royal Fusiliers). He died 30 May 1919 and is buried at the Ladywell Cemetery in London. The Commonwealth War Graves Commission website shows his parents as Edward and Clara Hunter, but the 1911 census shows Clara as a widow and living at 5 Albion Place, Sheerness. Besides Thomas, she had three other sons, Edward, William, and Alfred, as well as daughters, Clara and Lilly.

Alfred had enlisted in the army on 6 April 1908 at Sheerness, and became a private (8956) in the 1st Battalion, Royal West Kent Regiment. He was awarded his Silver War Badge and certificate, No. 251631, on 22 October 1917 after having being medically discharged from the army on 5 September 1917 for no longer being physically fit for war service due to a gunshot wound to his right arm and elbow joint.

William Webster Dennison was an engine room artificer 2nd class (271982) in the Royal Navy, serving on board HMS *Fandango* when he was killed by a mine explosion in the Dvina River at Archangel in North Russia on 3 July 1919. The *Fandango* was one of the ships sent to Russia by Churchill to prevent the Bolsheviks from capturing the armaments that were stockpiled there. This made William one of the last, if not *the* last, member of Britain's Armed Forces to be killed on active service during the First World War. His body was not recovered and his name is commemorated on the Chatham Memorial. His widow was living at 29 Ranelagh Road, Sheerness, at the time of his death.

H. Walker was a sergeant (208018) in the 108 Squadron, Royal Air Force, when he died on 20 February 1919. The squadron originated with the Royal Flying Corps and was formed at Stonehenge in November 1917. It subsequently moved on to Dunkirk and ended up at Bisseghem in Belgium, where it remained until it was disbanded in July 1919. He is buried at the Charleroi Communal Cemetery which is situated in the Hainaut region of Belgium. His widow, Mrs M. Walker, lived at Swanley Farm, Eastchurch, Sheerness.

William Edward Chaplin was 28 years of age and a gunner (65716) in the 99th Siege Battery, Royal Garrison Artillery, when he died on 28 April 1919. He had been wounded while serving on the Western Front as a result of a German gas attack and sent home to England where he died at the Military Garrison Hospital in Sheerness. Before the war he had been employed as a gas fitter by the Sheerness Gas Company. He is buried at the Sheerness Cemetery. After the war his parents, Joseph and Eliza, lived at 21 Harris Road, Mile Town, but at the time of the 1911 census they lived at 108 High Street, Mile Town, with William and their other son Alfred, who was five years older than William. Alfred was a labourer, but I could find no record of him having served in the armed forces during the war.

Ada Emeline Martin died on 30 April 1919. I mentioned her earlier, under the heading of Blue Town.

George Daniel Wood was 32 years of age and a staff sergeant (T/465) in the Royal Army Ordnance Corps when he died on 20 September 1919 at Shorncliffe Camp Sandgate. Having already been in the army before war had broken out, he had previously been wounded in 1915. He was buried at the Sheerness Cemetery. George's parents, George and Agnes, lived at 111 Alexander Road, Sheerness. They had six other children: sons William, Harry and Arthur, and daughters Nellie, Ethel and Isabel.

Herbert James Record was 31 years of age and a private (82127) in the 75th Battalion, Machine Gun Corps. He arrived in Alexandria on 7 June 1917 and a month later had been admitted to hospital for five days suffering with diarrhoea, as he no doubt struggled to adapt to his new environment. He died of bronchial pneumonia on 18 February 1919 after once again having been admitted to hospital (14th Stationary Hospital) five days earlier. The following is taken from the medical case sheet attached to Herbert's Army service record:

> *13-2-19 – Admitted with history of pains in head during past four days. Aching all over today, and fever. History of having had frequent attacks of Malaria, but doesn't know of what variety. Temperature on admission 100. e.t. 102.*
> *14-2-19 – Temperature 98.4, feels well.*
> *15-2-19 – Temperature 100. Blood film sent to the laboratory and returned as 'Negative for Parasites'. No cough.*
> *No physical signs in chest. Patient continually mutters to*

himself, but when spoken to is quite sensible. Place on Quin. Sulph. gr. x. t.d.s.

16-2-19 – Temperature down. Seems better. Taking nourishment well.

17-2-19 - Morning temp. 98.4. Evening temp. 102.6. Very cyanosed. Semi-conscious. Blood film returned from laboratory as 'negative'.

18-2-19 – The patient died at 6.30 am, February 18th 1919. Post Mortem.

Lungs healthy. Pleural cavities contain no fluid. Heart much dilated and filled with post-mortem clot, but healthy. Spleen congested but not enlarged. Liver congested. Kidney's healthy. Peritoneal cavity healthy. Smear from spleen found negative for pigment or parasites.

Death was due to Pyrexia of unknown origin contracted on active service, and due to such service.

I O G Steward
Captain RAMC
Medical Officer in charge 'C' Ward
24th Stationary Hospital
Egyptian Expeditionary Force.

He is buried at the Kantara War Memorial Cemetery, which is situated on the eastern side of the Suez Canal, about 160 kilometres from Cairo. He had enlisted at Bromley on 12 December 1915, initially being allocated as a private (G/11956) in the 3rd Battalion, The Buffs (East Kent Regiment), with whom he was with for the first four months of his military service. His army service record showed that he was married with one child, Nora, and that before enlisting he had been a butcher, living at 6 Spring Cottages, St Mary Cray, Kent. A second child, Ethel, was born nine months after he enlisted. Having been placed on the Army Reserve to start with, he wasn't in fact mobilized until 15 August 1916. While on the Army Reserve, Herbert had appeared before the Bromley Rural Military Tribunal on 25 May 1916 in an attempt at being exempted from military service. The application was made through his employer, The London Central Meat Co. Ltd, on the following grounds:

> *(1) The man's occupation is necessary to the inhabitants of the District, and the business is essential to the domestic needs of the immediate community. His occupation has previously been certified by a Government Department to be work of National Importance.*
> *(2) He is manager of the Branch shop of our Company at 2 Mary Ann Terrace, High Street, St Mary Cray.*
> *(3) It is impossible to replace him owing to the shortage of labour.*
> *(4) We have offered every facility for our employees to enlist, and over 380 of our men in different parts of the country have joined His Majesty's Forces, being 50% of our employees of military age. Through this we have already been compelled to close 85 Branches.*
>
> *We are satisfied to have one man only for each shop, but if we are not allowed this, our shops must be closed and <u>financial ruin will follow for this Company</u>, therefore robbing the state of considerable revenue in rates and taxes.*
>
> *In the event of this man leaving our employ we undertake to advise the Recruiting Officer.*

The application for a certificate of exemption was rejected, a decision which he decided to appeal. The hearing for this appeal was heard at 10 am on 25 July 1916 at the West Kent Appeal Tribunal, Sessions House, in Maidstone. After having considered Herbert's appeal, the tribunal dismissed it. After the war the government ordered local authorities to destroy all documentation in their possession relating to military tribunals, so to actually come across such documentation was an absolute privilege. Herbert's parents, John (a bricklayer) and Eliza, had before the war lived at 143a High Street in Sheerness, but by the time Herbert had enlisted in the army, they had moved to 18 Rose Street, Sheerness. Herbert's wife Winnifred, whom he had married on 26 November 1912, initially lived at 6 Spring Cottages, St Mary Cray, before later moving to 120 Grange Road, Gillingham, Kent. Herbert had three brothers, John, who was a year older than him, along with Thomas and William. He also had three sisters, Matilda, Eliza and Amelia.

Arthur Thomas Fisher was 38 years of age and a private (23185) in the 10th (Prince of Wales's Own Royal) Hussars, when he died of his wounds received during the fighting of the Second Battle of the Somme, on 12 June 1919. He is buried at the Sheerness Cemetery. He had also seen service during the South African War of 1899-1902. He was a married man whose wife Estella lived at 1 Pleasant Cottage, East Half Way House, Sheerness.

William James Warren was 40 years of age and a skipper in the Royal Navy Reserve serving with HMS *Arctic Whale* when he died on 23 November 1919. He is buried at the Scartho Road Cemetery in Grimsby. The *Arctic Whale* served as a coastal anti-submarine escort throughout most of the war. It served in the Second World War as HMS *Bermudian*. William's parents, John and Sarah, lived in Minster on the Isle of Sheppey, while his wife Rebecca lived at 20 Clyde Street, Grimsby.

His elder brother John Thomas Warren also served in the Royal Navy during the war, having enlisted on 27 September 1910 as an able seaman (187936). He was finally demobbed on 3 March 1919, having served on numerous different vessels.

Edwin Charles Watson was 30 years of age and a private (25432) in the 1st (Garrison) Battalion, Suffolk Regiment, but transferred to the 602nd Home Service Employment Company, Labour Corps, as Private (323821). He died on 25 March 1919 and is buried at Gravesend Cemetery. His wife lived at 6 Gordon Avenue, Queenborough.

Besides families and friends having to cope with their pain and sadness at still losing loved ones to the war months after it had officially come to an end, the peace and tranquillity which came with normality was what people now wanted. For the first time in more than four years, the war was no longer the main topic of conversation. Here are a few examples of that normality that was gradually creeping back in to society.

For one Isle of Sheppey resident, 1919 got off to a better than expected start. Douglas Peter Jones, who was a 2nd lieutenant in the Rifle Brigade, had appealed against a judgement which had originally been made against him at the Wycombe County Bench in July 1918, directing that he was the father of a child born to Gundred Mary Newton of Wycombe Heath, an allegation which he had always vehemently denied. Part of the order meant that he had to pay Miss Newton five shillings a week for the upkeep of the child. His argument was that as the unnamed child in question wasn't his, he shouldn't be paying a single penny to Miss Newton. After strong arguments had been put forward by his barrister, Sir Ryland Adkins, Jones had to sit and wait while the judge, Sir Denham Warmington, fully digested both sides of the argument. He found in his favour, and set aside the original order that had been handed out by the Wycombe County Bench.

On Saturday, 12 April 1919, Whitstable played an away fixture against Sheppey United in a friendly football match. The match eventually ended up as a 1-1 draw. Sheppey fielded a relatively strong team in the circumstances, which included several players who usually played for teams in the Southern League. Whitstable were without their star striker in Newman, but had in his place Paisley, who lined up in the inside left position. The pitch was in good condition which allowed both teams to play an attractive attacking style of football, which was just what the large crowd of loyal supporters, from both sides, wanted to see. Sheppey quickly gained the upper hand, and in the early stages of the match Whitstable's goalkeeper, Saddleton, kept his side in the game with several fine saves, which prevented Sheppey from gaining a lead. The longer the game continued, the more it became an exciting end-to-end battle, with both goalkeepers proving their worth. All of Whitstable's forwards, in particular Rock, Philipps and Paisley, were raining down shots on the Sheppey goal, but a combination of missed chances, the crossbar and fine saves by the Sheppey goalkeeper, meant their hard work was to no avail. The game continued to ebb and flow, with Sheppey being awarded a penalty just before the stroke of half time after the Whitstable defender, Cornford, brought down Sheppey's inside left in the penalty area. The same player stepped up to take the spot kick, which was majestically saved by Saddleton, which kept the score at 0-0 at the interval. The first twenty minutes after the break saw the game played at an almost frenetic pace, with both sides attacking one moment and then defending the next. It was during this period of play, and after a quick interchange between Rock and Paisley, that the latter opened the scoring for the visitors with a low cross shot which beat the Sheppey goalkeeper in the far corner of the goal. This appeared to spur on Sheppey more than it did their visitors, although the Whitstable defence, which was superbly marshalled by Saddleton, held firm. But in the very last minute of the game, after a bit of a goalmouth scramble, the ball was bundled across the line and Sheppey had won themselves a well-deserved draw.

Some of the men who had taken part in the fighting were putting the wartime skills that they had learnt to good use. On Friday, 18 April 1919, Major J.C.P. Wood piloted a Short biplane from Eastchurch on the Isle of Sheppey to Limerick in Ireland. His navigator and companion for the flight was Captain Wyllie. Both men had served in the Royal Flying Corps and the Royal Air Force during the war. From Limerick they intended flying across the Atlantic, with their final destination being Newfoundland. Their Atlantic flight attempt was part of a race. Another of those ex-Royal Air Force aviators who was taking part was a Captain W.R. Curtis, who flew a biplane from the Alliance Aeroplane Company Limited. Major Wood's biplane fell into the Irish Sea, but he was rescued, allegedly by picnickers, and lived until 1970.

By August 1919 the war was well and truly over, with more and more military establishments throughout the United Kingdom being relinquished by the different military authorities as they were now surplus to requirements. This included military training camps, prisoner of war camps, airfields and other aeronautical wartime

Balloonists preparing to take off.

establishments, such as the Kite Balloon base at Sheerness which covered a seventy-five-acre site south of the dockyard at Sheerness. Many of the fields were returned to their pre-war use of farming.

The same month saw the cancellation of the orders put in place in March 1918 under the Defence of the Realm Regulations, by Admiral Sir Doveton Sturdee who was the commander-in-chief at the Nore, prohibiting civilian or any other unauthorised approach to the air stations at Eastchurch and Leysdown, as well as the Kite Balloon base.

The Kite Balloon Base was used for the advanced training of naval observers who would eventually work high up in the balloons. Before arriving at the No.1 Balloon Training Base, Sheerness, the cadets would have already successfully completed their initial training course at Roehampton. The base was home to 174 trainers and staff, which allowed for 132 officers to be trained at any given time. The accommodation was relatively sparse and consisted of large tents which wouldn't have made for a totally comfortable living environment during the colder winter months, especially as

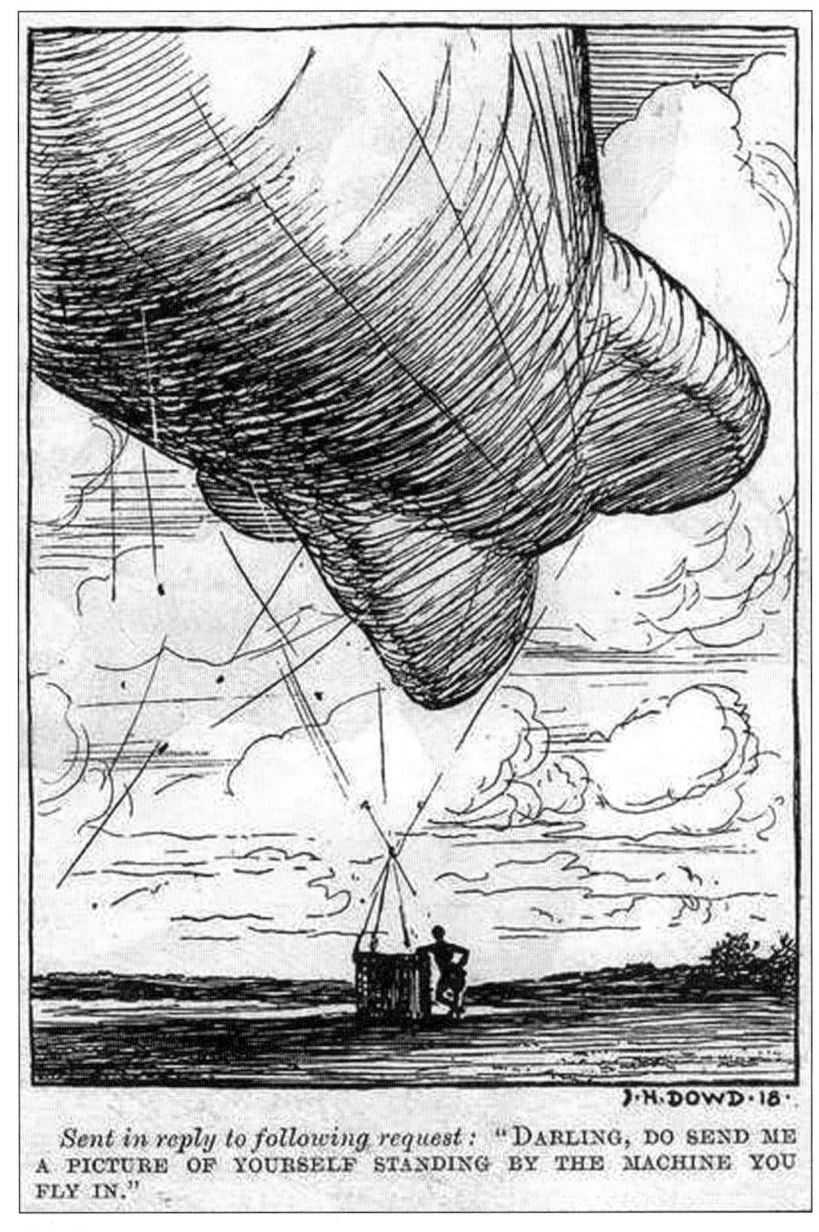

Sent in reply to following request: "DARLING, DO SEND ME A PICTURE OF YOURSELF STANDING BY THE MACHINE YOU FLY IN."

Punch cartoon.

Two-man crew preparing to take off. (fold3.com)

they were right on the coast. The balloons that were used for the training were kept in five large canvas-covered sheds.

Nearly all of those who were trained as balloon observers were of officer rank. The job was not for the faint-hearted, not only because of their vulnerability to enemy aircraft, but because of the heights that the balloons could be deployed at, and the weather could be inclement to say the least. The men wore padded coveralls, sheepskin hats and gloves.

Once operational an observer could spend hours high in the skies which, in the early years of their use, was a solitary existence. This was for a sound operational reason: the earlier balloons were not that substantial and with only one man in the balloon basket they could reach much greater heights than with two. By June 1916, the balloons were of a much better design, which allowed for two-man crews. Thankfully all of the observers had the luxury of wearing parachutes, which meant that their chances of survival were greater than most aircraft pilots, who didn't tend to wear them. The majority of balloon losses were down to enemy aircraft attacks, although some of them were also brought down by artillery fire. The balloons were provided with some protection in the form of machine gunners or anti-aircraft guns on the ground below. With the balloons being capable of reaching heights of over 3,500 feet, they were an extremely useful tool for both sides to use, being able to provide up-to-date intelligence of enemy movements, troop numbers and artillery locations, as well as gathering meteorological information. Each side went to great lengths to destroy any enemy balloons that they saw observing their location or operations. The crews were classed as Company or Wing staff, or Section staff. Those officers, like Flight Sub-Lieutenant Sydney Harry Gudgin, who were trained in meteorology, were part of the former group. Meteorological data was collected at two-hourly intervals and was then telephoned to the relevant headquarters three times a day, in an effort to provide some kind of weather forecast.

The original make-up of one of these groups was a balloon section, which consisted of one balloon, and each balloon company

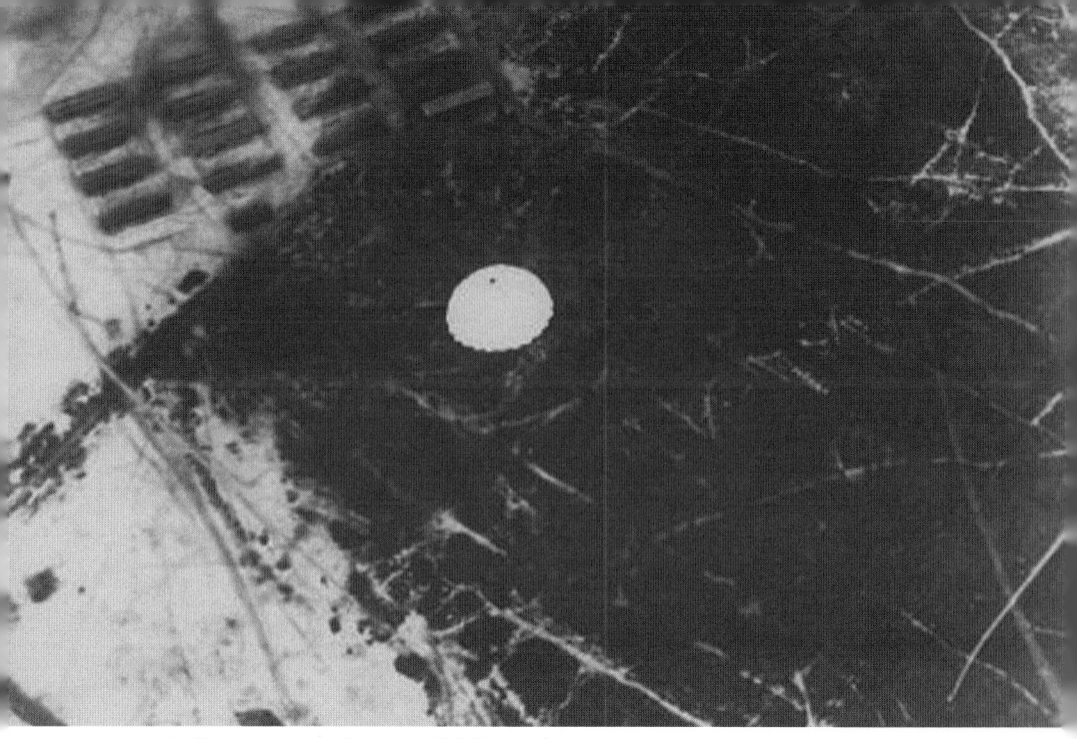

Balloonist parachuting. (fold3.com)

consisted of two sections, although these figures were increased after June 1917. The Kite Balloon Base remained open until the signing of the Armistice, when it was closed. It was handed back to the Admiralty in September 1919.

A hearing took place at the King's Bench on Monday, 27 October 1919, which saw a nurse seek damages from a Sheerness Justice of the Peace for an alleged slander he had made against her during a public meeting. Miss Mary Ruth Maunders, a nurse, of Hill House, Ramsgate, sued Mr Charles Ingleton JP for comments he made at a meeting of the Sheppey Rural District Council at which a large number of members of the public were present. Mr Ingleton had said of Miss Maunders, 'She is not a fit and proper person to take charge of a fever isolation hospital.' Mr Ingleton denied having spoken the alleged words, but then confusingly and somewhat contradictorily added that if he had in fact said what was alleged then he had done so on what he called a 'privileged occasion' and that it would have been said 'without malice'. Miss Maunders had been mentioned in despatches during her wartime service for her meritorious conduct. Under cross-examination by council for Mr Ingleton, she denied that complaints in regard to unruly patients had been made against her. She admitted that it was true that she had called the Master of the Sheerness Workhouse a liar and a worm (to the amusement of those present in court). Mr Ingleton, a local man who was born in Minster, was a farmer who lived with his wife Fanny, to whom he had been married for 47 years, at Borstal Lodge, Minster. Despite their years of wedded bliss, the marriage had not been blessed with any children. Miss Maunders was 39 years of age in 1919. The 1911 census recorded that she was the nursing superintendent at the Workhouse Infirmary in Kidderminster. I have not been able to find out how this case was concluded.

On Monday, 24 November 1919, a conference took place at Sittingbourne of the local authorities from the Sheppey and Sittingbourne Districts. The meeting was called by Kent County Council to ascertain the views of the district on the best means of improving access to the Isle of Sheppey. At the time the only connection between the island and the mainland was the bridge at Kings Ferry, which carried a single line of rails and a road. Because of the increase in the output of the Kent coal industry, and the importance of Queenborough as a port and manufacturing centre, the town's mayor stated that in his opinion the bridge which they had was outdated and not suited to the increased needs that were being placed upon it. The option favoured by most local residents, including the Admiralty, was a new road and rail bridge at Elmley Ferry, near Sittingbourne, which would have linked up with a projected railway across Kent into Sussex, which would in turn free up the Swale traffic. The delegation from Sheerness, somewhat surprisingly, voted to keep the bridge that was already in place, and simply repair and improve it. After all concerned had their say, a decision was taken to send a deputation to the Ministry of Transport to see what could be expected in the way of central financial support for each of the suggested schemes.

In 1920 a further 14,633 Britons who had served their King and Country during the First World War died as a result of the wounds they had received on active service or from illness. Two of these men had connections with the Isle of Sheppey.

James Thomas Munn (mentioned above), was a petty officer stoker (K/2715) and was serving on board HMS *Godetia* when he died on 22 April 1920.

John Russell Blinch, Distinguished Service Medal, had enlisted on 1 July 1914 and went on to become a chief petty officer (187787) in the Royal Navy serving on board HMS *Botha* when he died 16 January 1920. John was awarded his DSM for services in destroyer and torpedo boat flotillas during the period ending 31 December 1917. His award was gazetted on 5 March 1918. John was already in the Royal Navy before the outbreak of the war. The 1911 census shows him serving on HMTB No. Xl at Stangate Creek in Sheerness. John died as a result of a problem with the anaesthetic used during an operation which he required to treat injuries he sustained after having being accidently knocked down by a motor vehicle. He is buried at Sheerness Cemetery on the isle of Sheppey. His widow, Mrs Mabel Blanch Blinch, lived at 27 St Vincent Terrace, Sheerness.

The last year that official records were kept which made a connection between somebody's service during the First World War and their subsequent death was 1921. By the end of that year a further 10,562 Britons were recorded as having died as a result of them having been in military service during the course of the First World War. Two of these had connections with the Isle of Sheppey.

Henry John Sewell, Distinguished Conduct Medal, Meritorious Service Medal, was 27 years of age and a lance sergeant (2306227) in the Wireless Company of the Royal Corps of Signals when he died on 6 March 1921. He is buried at the Cairo War Memorial Cemetery. His mother, Mrs E. Sewell, lived at 65 Invicta Road, Sheerness.

William Swift Wade was 42 years of age and a sergeant (4523719) in the 1st Battalion, West Yorkshire Regiment (Prince of Wales's Own), when he died on 27 August 1921. He was a holder of the Army's Long Service and Good Conduct Medal. He is buried at the All Saints Churchyard Extension in Walton-on-the-Naze. His late father, John William Swift Wade, was from Sheerness, while at the end of the war, William's widow, Lizzie, was living at 1 Percival Villas, Walton-on-the-Naze, Essex.

The war was now well and truly over and the normality of everyday life, or the post-war version of it, was back in full swing. Many more people would continue to die as a result of the war, while some of those who had survived would never truly get over their involvement in it and the loss of their comrades and friends.

Sources

1914-1918.net
ancestry.co.uk
britishnewspaperarchive.co.uk
clydesite.co.uk
cwgc.co.uk
digplanet.com
invisionzone.com
kenthistoryforum.co.uk
naval-history.net
navymuseum.co.nz
sheppeywebsite.co.uk
spartacus-educational.com
uboat.net
wartimememoriesproject.com
Wikipedia
wrecksite.eu (Jan Lettens)

Index

Actaeon, HMS, 80, 94–5
Allen, William, 117
Allison, Henry William, 83–4, 127, 131
Anderson, John, 73
Anderson, Samuel, 81, 131
Argent, John William, 30, 127
Ashenden, Archibald Herbert, 112, 127
Attew, Robert, 62

Bailey, Frederick J., 60, 130
Balloon Training Base, 148, 151–2
Barbed Wire Island, 10, 27
Barden, Ida, 46
Barker, Richard George, 92
Bass, William Reuben, 110, 128, 133
Batchelor, Thomas Robert, 110–11, 128, 133
Batt, Albert, 30–1
Battles,
  Aisne, 16
  Albert, 56, 105
  Arras, 80, 100
  Cambrai, 113–14
  Gallipoli, 27
  Gaza, 125–6
  Jutland, 54, 107
  Loos, 19
  Lys, 98–9
  Marne, 16, 102–103
  Mons, 16–17
  Neuve Chapelle, 19, 27, 49–50
  Passchendaele, 80
  Second Ypres, 27
  Somme, 55–7, 64, 67, 69, 78, 105, 123, 145
  Verdun, 55
Beaumont, Charles, 37
Beeston, Thomas, 91
Bentley, Ernest, 68
Bird, William, 76
Black, Capt Eric, 33
Blake, John Henry, 52–3
Blinch, John Russell, 154
Bolton, William Alfred, 112–13
Boother, James Daniel, 16, 18, 125, 134
Bromley, John Richard, 35, 128
Brown, Robert, 139
Brunger, William George, 28
Budd, Sgt Albert Cosham, 23
Bulwark, HMS, 23–4, 43
Bull, George Joseph, 47–8
Bull, William Edward, 47–8
Bushell, Robert Lewis, 103
Butler, Charles Edward, 109, 128

Carpenter, Ernest George, 18, 128
Carroll, Henry John, 82–3, 128, 132
Caston, Hugh Charles, 88–90

Castle, William Henry, 36, 123, 130
Chaplin, William Edward, 134, 141
Chave, Walter J., 75–6
Clarke, Edward Charles, 118, 120
Cleeve, Richard, 71
Conroy, Henry Ernest, 57, 128, 134
Copland, Henry Townsend, 51
Copland, John, 50
Copland, Mary Jane, 50
Copland, William Shrubsole, 51
Cox, Frederick George, 31, 128, 132
Cox, Frederick William, 84
Cox, George Thomas, 48–50
Crampin, Alexander John, 123, 130, 134

Davie, George, 128, 134, 140
Davis, Ernest Edward, 102, 128, 134
Day, William Ewart Gladstone, 23
Deadman, E.A., 58–9, 125
Dennison, William Webster, 128, 141
Dryer, Harry, 80–1, 128, 132
Duffy, Fred Goodlad, 23
Dye, Alfred, 48–9

Ernst, Karl Gustav, 20

Fisher, Arthur Thomas, 128, 145

Fittall, William Thomas, 128, 139
Fitch, Arthur John, 91
Fitzpatrick, Rev H.P., 39

George, Ernest Foster, 32, 128
Gordon, Robert, 32, 128, 134
Green, George, 72

Hammett, Leonard, 83, 128, 133
Hamnett, Arthur Septimus, 31–2, 129
Hancock, Harold Claude, 129, 134, 139
Hardy, George, 34
Hawes, Samuel H., 80, 136
Hogben, Frederick, 78, 134
Hogben, Stephen Robert, 79
Hogben, William, 34–5, 129, 134
Holmes, Edwin Charles, 107, 110
Hopkins, George Thomas, 108
Horswell, Charles, 109, 129, 134
Howard, George Robert, 111, 129
Howard, John George, 129, 134, 137–8
Howting, Edward, 98–9
Howting, William, 121, 124

Jeans, John Edwin Henry, 125, 127
Jempson, Charles, 110, 129, 134
Johnson, George Henry, 51
Johnson, William, 23

INDEX

Ketley, Harold Norman, 67
King, John Edward, 101, 129
Knowler, George Edward, 37

Lamb, Frank Valentine, 84–5, 129, 133
Ledger, Harry, 127, 134
Levy, Harold George, 112, 129
Losel, Franz Heinrich, 13–14
Lucas, William George, 91
Lynch, Jeremiah, 87, 129, 133

Macdonald, Alexander, 58, 135
Marshall, George Patrick, 45
Marshall, Stephen Frederick, 23
Martin, Ada Emeline, 125, 142
Middlesex Regiment, 15, 68, 88, 99, 102, 108, 139
Miles, Henry William, 107, 113, 123
Moore-Brabazon, Lord, 10
Munn, James Thomas, 124, 131, 134
Murby, Alonzo, 129, 139–40
Murdock, Albert Victor, 35–6, 122, 124, 135

Netley Hospital *see* Royal Victoria Hospital
Newman, Alfred John William, 36, 46, 124
Norman, George Ernest James, 61–2, 124

Pack, Frederick, 127, 135
Packer, George Arthur, 59, 125
Paston, George Thomas, 35, 129, 133

Percival, Alfred Charles, 19, 21, 135
Phillips, George, 125
Pitter, Charles, 23
Potter, Victor, 43–4, 46
Prendergast, Capt, 20–1
Princess Irene, HMS, 28, 35–6, 41–5, 46, 101, 131, 136
Purdy, Thomas Henry, 35, 129, 133

Record, Herbert James, 142
Reed, William John Henry, 32
Richardson, George, 31
Robson, Arthur Albert, 65
Royal Aero Club, 11, 93
Royal Victoria Hospital, 59, 89–90
Runham, Ernest Henry, 67

Samson, Lt Charles Rumney, 10
Saunders, Frederick Charles, 35, 118, 129, 135
Screapige, 7
Sellen, Alfred William, 37
Sellen, James Alfred, 99, 129, 135
Sellen, James Richard, 140
Sewell, Henry John, 129, 154
Sharland, Arthur, 101, 130, 135
Sheerness War Memorial, 131–2
Shrubsole, James, 56, 123–4
Sims, Walter Charles, 123
Sole, Edward, 63, 135
Spackman, Frederick Charles, 23
Steele, Ernest, 28–9, 130
Stickings, Alfred Ernest, 124
Stone, David, 64

Stone, Thomas A., 113, 130
Strait, James, 23
Stroud, Norman, 23
Sugg, James Henry, 63–4, 135
Sullivan, Edwin Austin, 32, 130

Thirkettle, Victor Arnold Norman, 130, 135, 139
Thompson, Edward, 31, 130
Turner, Edward Charles, 102
Turner, George James, 43–4, 46

Underdown, Thomas Rouse, 102, 131

Vaughan, William M.J., 51–2, 58

Wade, William Swift, 130, 154
Warde, Chief Constable of Kent, 21
Warren, John Thomas, 123, 131, 145
Warren, William James, 145
Watson, Edwin Charles, 145
Westbrook, Henry, 62, 135
Whiddett, Frank, 87
Whish, John Kenneth Tulloch, 19–20, 124
Whiting, Albert C., 84, 130, 135
Wilcocks, Robert, 85, 125, 130
Wildfire, HMS, 83, 117
Wilson, Alexander Mackintosh, 32–4, 130, 133
Wilson, Woodrow, 55
Wood, Frederick S., 37–8
Wood, George Daniel, 133, 142
Wood, Richard, 46, 101, 130
Wright, Harold James, 43

Yates, George Thomas, 105, 124
Young, Charles Sidney, 136, 138